The LITTLE SUBLIME COMEDY

The LITTLE SUBLIME COMEDY

JOHN GALLAS

CARCANET PRESS · MMXVII

First published in Great Britain in 2017
by CARCANET PRESS LTD
Alliance House, 30 Cross Street, Manchester M2 7AQ
www.carcanet.co.uk

A CIP catalogue record for this book is available
from the British Library: ISBN 9781784104740.

Book design: Luke Allan.
Printed and bound in England by SRP Ltd.

Supported using public funding by
ARTS COUNCIL
ENGLAND

I

THE BAD PLACE

I

THE BAD PLACE

SONG 1 · *the novice lies upon a sunny mountain above Lake Rotoiti / he slumbers
amidst sweet nature's noises and the issues of onan*

Wanked warm on the mountainside,
on a sunny *hunangāmoho* palliasse,
mānuka high at my headwards,
down we watched, the trees and me,
a while the shining still-sweet Rotoiti water
in its bice and flicker-banked sink
beneath the labour-level sun.

No wonder then snooze and slumber in me,
honeying the eyesoft muck within
with sunny rheum.

No wonder then the keas' grating calm,
the koromikos' bottled gongs,
the mozzies' buzzy yaws,
the clouds' mutewhite beautbright
sliding slow.

And my seed in my hip,
its separate milk
running
at the mouth of earth.

SONG 2 · *a terrible beast appears at the edge of his snoozing vision / which is a vegetable sheep / the novice apprehends an awful mortality in its eye*

And then, upon a sudden
bomp, fuck me, am I not
eye-to-eye, I am not a foot off
with this exact vegetable ram!
A soft white bristle-back slumbery thing,
hunched blurry and bump on the earth,
woolly with white-flower and leaf-flesh.

A panting cloud-accordion
as I saw it in the blue above.

There its melancholy glue-lens:
there, ah! tell me not it knows not death,
its own end, and ours, and everything,
for it stank there,
sunning its rank-rot,
stagnant and wheezingfast,
bewildering about it all,
and its fair snout and all at the end.

And I too in its eye afloat
with the world in a glass.

Dear companionable soul.

SONG 3 · *the first encounter with Mr Beckett / who ascends the mountain track into view in some usual dress and boots*

And then hard upon (and I for a sec
quite summer-birdwit, drowsing
on warmish whispers)
as if that were not enough for a sunny day,
comes first a hat –

serviceable, but not quite the thing –
to be followed anon by
spectacles, saucers and glass, one pair,
heliographing all over the bloody show,
that seemed two little suns
rising from tussock, and next,
after,
a fawn turtleneck,
and a black *something* mostly the rest rising,
maybe a suit I think,
which would fit, following that is,
and a little shining, with the shoes surely
of a fashion for the feet
of a man
of the happy strenuous
walking kind, but hid
at their ends notwithstanding
in scree-shambles,
erosion, down-dust,
dormant colluvial fans,
and glorious nature's weed.

SONG 4 · *the novice meets Mr Beckett / he questions himself concerning the purpose of this visit / Mr B is not pleased to be out / the novice rises*

Who are you, I sang, still from the supine,
that comes to my dream if it is one,
summer and pleased with my own,
waking or sleeping if it is or not,
trickling scree on the mountainside
above the lapis lake I like so well?

Ha, it replied, whattering to a stop.
It's your Saaaam.

Baa. The little white bleaty flowers.

II

He halted upon the horizon hexactly.
I hastened my flies to their buttons.
Shall I cry now immediately lead on,
I considered,
or pause or linger,
or bask even
at the edge of this intelligence
driven betwixt heav'n and earth
with the fixture of an idea of marble perhaps?

I am damned lost and what vile vicissitudes,
it growled.
Though it should be surely you.

I rose from my silly straws
like a falling plank
reversi.

SONG 5 · *Mr B leads the novice into the sky upon the promise of visiting eternity*

Is this the resurrection
that I cannot believe in? I cried,
with a small twang to the absolute upright.

Resurrection be damned, said Sam.
Come, and we shall see anon,
hermeneutically,
the abode where lost bodies roam
in the lovely dispensation
of supernal mechanics.
It is just up there,
above us somewhere if you will.

He waved his arm into the sky,
which was entirely blue,
except for the small dibbling clouds.

Will?

I took his wearied gall-scuff hand,
and out we stepped *whoa!*
off the pittering fall of the mountain,
over the brightblue lay of the lake,
I a little damp *here*, about the pocket,

off our whenua
and into the sky.

SONG 6 · *the novice describes the meticulous exactitude of eternity / where it is / how it moves / and that it is made of each day done forever held in recurrence / and visible to those properly equipped*

Shall I tell you, ye souls of this world,
of the ichnographic air?
It is indescribable, unfortunately.

That if we had not pursued particularly
upon the collimations that we did,
that we should not have arrived at the precincts
that we have?

That hangs there, ah, patulous
past Te Mangōroa,
at the velocity of *p* there
(wherever *there* was [or *is*], though exactly indeed
it certainly *was* [or *is*] {which cannot be everywhere
qua everywhere, as some misportion of space
must be possessed, as some catenation of time too,
to the paths, or ways, or *directions* indeed
of getting there, and the period took}),
consequent to the above,
each day that has, to our mean understanding,
(as mean shall I say as a quarterglass merely a day,
and our sipping care not to spill for very fear of it)

13

done, in its goddamned entire entirety,
and every detail to the uttermost and the utterleast,
at the inspection of who
may attain the acceleration,
and the perspicacity,
and the way,
and the path (or the path),
and the *direction* (or the *direction*),
to find it,
keep up beside it,

and have eyes to see?

SONG 7 · *they arrive, after a relative flight, at The Bad Place / a description of its five-dimensional and interminable increase*

We did not flee, we did not fly,
But in the twinkling of an eye
Became another place,
Despitto Time and Space.

Hello, here it comes, said Sam.

We did not light, we did not land,
But hovered in the integrand,
Bright as titiwai,
Shiftless as the sky.

And may they be lost who have lived?
I asked. To which he said, Behold!
See, they are lost and they live!

This is a Bad Place.

And each day all and ever done I saw
was a white room,
even from end to the end of time,

which there is not, with a white window,
each fixed next to the next,
and on and on, about and about,
and beyond all and each,

pale cities breeding on each preterite mo,
in five degrees, being thus: A in a line,
B upon a surface, C within a space,
D tesseractually, E additionally a wing,
so to speak, made upon the passing time,
that is to be understood passing,
that is *going by* and not in the least *going away*,
possessing only a present
in which to damn one's self.

SONG 8 · *they reach Wing 1, where the Falsely Contented must forever run against time in their hopeless desire to be saved in another day / the novice recognises A, and asks to go down and speak to him*

Why this is hell, nor am I out of it.
Where are you damned?

And the milk air's mouth,
and the endless city's burgeoning,
and its endless faring,
and no hope to go back.

Come and look, said Sam.
Some are fitted with a sliding extension.

And I saw the slightly damned
seeking in atomic winds their *there*,
to wind there their *them* back,
back try back breaststroke and sprint
and again run at it and again at it
and again again again again at it
again to gain a different day,

the thud of bodies near no door,
in white rooms seeking a door
to a different day.

Shall we take the lift down? said Sam.
I hung in his hand.
I would speak with one, who I saw was A
from the ski-school of my holidays.

The possibility of my word
whispered a wandering veil of shade,
like soupsteam, along their hopeless cell.

Ah, cried some, do you think of spending time among us?
Their voice, no voice, a sylkothread white of some soul
let down and the voice near no door.

Go down to him sure, said dear Sam.

SONG 9 · *the novice nervously descends / Wing 1 described / the novice speaks to*
A and sees for himself the hopeless struggle to go backwards

So and I did.
Unsteady, I asked, might I fall,
tripping tentative from his brotherly grip
down the long white ceiling
to the bloody long white toilet.

All that fall, said Sam, may be caught.

A landscape of furnishings loomed
like a medley of cow positions in a mist;
here a bedside lamp, there a sofa for two,
and yonder a nest of acrylic tables.

Of course, called the faintering master's eloquence now,
caught falling, yes, they may not be raised

once more to their former eminence,
but they can be caught, at least.
It's a fair arrangement.

Safe from the torment's unturning tide,
I billowed down in my crisp, embarrassed pants.

'Hiyotoho! You that are there,
that cannot relive this day!
A!'

A red grill-apron knotted up his knees
where he stumbled and clawed for advancement,
but could not beyond the tables.

I am A, he wept,
not striving to amend my unthinking hour,
but seeking familiar comfort elsewhere,
where I always was.
I took, contented, what was given me:
have pity on my agony!

The periwigged lamp,
longing to be knocked arse over tit,
encouraged his effort in vain.

This was their moment.

SONG 10 · *they climb to the kitchen of Wing 1 / the lonely dancers / they reach the bedroom / the novice speaks without comfort to the truckled woman / they prepare to descend to Wing 2*

We clambered the air to the kitchen.

These are the souls that never lived, said Sam,
that dance in the trough of time.

It was a kind of Twist,
on bottles of water,
lurching at plastic cobblestones,
and cushioned from fall always.

I am B, cried a girl
with fingers areach at my whispering shadow.
Lend me your phone.
God, I am alone.

We glid up the carpeted stair
to a bedroom in white with white,
and the tiles weeping rusted globs
at balls and bars of chrome
that lay still at the wardrobe's mouth.

Why am I here? called a bedcapped whitely
woman from the bed.
Oh, one of you comes here not dead!
What will become of me, say?
What will become of me, pray?

Why nothing, my lady, will come of you,
but only this that you are,
for this is forever and all.

The lift is usefully near, said Sam
and offered his arm.
You know, he sighed aside,
I envy her almost.

SONG 11 · *they journey to Wing 2 where the selfish Liars, Deceivers and Flatterers sit about a fondue table fixed upon each others' hearts / the novice speaks to C, D and E*

Going down.
There was a fatuous little light that said 2.

Second floor! cried Sam,
where a stain of pissyellow
dreeped in the opening lift,
and our order of oxygen.

Liars, Deceivers and Flatterers!
Those general bastards.

We came to a soft-hissing halt here
at its most orrible, and ascended a little stair
to the spattered, infinite-almost box
of stillness, each-agony, and blood.

Amongst the million in this stained diningroom
crouched three that I knew.
What, C! D! and E!
Are you here! At the round-revolving tabletop,
weaving and turning, turning and weaving
the great sulphur-stained silver kettles
farting fondue about their knit-pictured jerseys
and their brylon skipants.

And there they will look, as the room sails,
silent and still in the merciless stars of infinite-gone,
at each others' hearts, who had lived by their own.

It is the silencing of silence,
at last and without end.
How are you here, who I knew,
and the lives of the parties?

SONG 12 · *how C passed by / the novice scolds her / how they must barf for each
earthly excuse / the liar D and the toady E / Mr B and the novice make for the lift*

She is here for the loss of a cold cold man,
She is here for the loss of a penny,
She is here for the loss of a lost old man,

She is here for the loss of many.

Clear a path for thy heart,
oh deceived deceiver:
for, see, it was not one life,
make what you can of it,
and damn the rest.

Here, haunted with baconbits, sisters of vomit,
spilled over teeth and tongue,
dropping in knitweave and nylon,
each a word that had been,
at the ting of a wetcheese fork.
For they have set their skins
aside for another:
her heart seen in the rent of a pullover
knitted with reindeer, and a wire-cuttered chest.

What did D do? Lied to be funny.
What did E do? Flattered for money.
Hearts of cheese.
Save me please.

Jesus, what a racket of peeled organs!
We slopped our mucal way
through lino and babycham
to the butchery lift.

O Beadalbane! O Tamburlaine!
O Charlemagne! O Aquitaine!
O the pain, O the pain.

Fucking nonsense, said Sam.
Let us descend.

To the whines of deflating flutes.

Christ! Sam leapt back
from the pus-oiled door
as it badbreath'd open.

Within was a man. Resplendent,
but for the bruisy tarnishings of his golden dress.
Ah, said Sam, collecting his dignities,
a new arrival. Shall we inspect his label?

It was tied to his quick with a piece of tinsel,
and flapped eager-doggily about his nether parts.
'A Bloody Great Liar', I read. It was the lift then,
first for a million years, up and down, up and down,
for him and the headphones glued to his ears.

And ever he will hear the only lie that matters.
Sam pressed the DOWN bulb.
And what is that? I said.
Take yourself for a small listen, said Sam.
He will thank you for it. The bastard.

We lowered through the universe,
and I shuffled nearer to the golden man.
The eyes had ceased to search.
I lifted one creamchrome podlet
a little off his face, with a small rip,
and laid my better ear to its meshy mouth.

Sooooon, soooooooooon – a round, merry voice it was –
this will end, this all will be over,
maybe so at the next supernatancy,
maybe upon the titubation following,
up and down up and down
sooooon sooooooooon it will end,
and the sunshine grass with your favourite daisies,

Bimbom the Donkey and tomatoes on toast,
maybe so upon this —

Clonk. We debouched in a nivosity,
and the door shut upon his golden earnings.

SONG 14 · *Wing 3 described / whiteness and fatal darts / they advance cautiously /*
they hide behind a stone and look for the Hypocrites, those of Bad Faith

This ghastly whiteness that we stepped out on unseen
was punctuated with fearful,
sudden, sharp, swift, whistling
commas, colons and semicolons.
There appeared to be no fullstops
as far as I could see.

As a matter of fact,
we could not tell what it was
that punctuated this ghastly whiteness,
but only that it was puncutated.
Exclamation mark.

And marks. Oh, what marks!

Get thee behind me, hissed Sam.
This is a kindness. Believe me.

We tippy-toed forward together,
I clinging to him and behind all week,
from etiolation to etiolation,
upon the Hypocrites, and their Bad Faith,

wherever they were.

Whizzzzz! Swisssssssh!
Swizzzz! Whisssssssh!
Splot! Split! Splat! Splet! Splut!

Aha! Sam inched behind an albescent boulder.
A rent in the cloud. Look. Can you bear it?

I strained my eyes upon cod-goggle proportions
and prepared my soul to be struck athwart
by the pity of it all,
when I could bloody make it out.

SONG 15 · *they observe the plain geography of Wing 3 / and see what is apparently*
a strange monster / which Mr B identifies

We cowered uninjurable
amongst the spunaway atoms
of a white metagalaxy.
Boulders, said Sam, cleaning his glasses
with a plain handkerchief.

We had, upon our sight then being suddenly
used to the darkness of whiteness,
a tolerable view of the intervening plain,
though the weather was changeable,
and whiteouts and brightbouts
followed hard upon one another
or did not and persisted
pretty much most of the time.

What is that? I asked Sam,
having glimpsed dashing about the fog
an awful, strange creature with six trotters
and unsuitable heads
in several directions at once.

That, answered my dear guide,
peering at the spectacle through his spectacles,
is a triumvirate of Vicious Pietists,
and there behind that bloody lunatic
the Kolkottan Tridentine –

ow! ouch!

Eek!

For he had seen them, and so had I,
punished.

SONG 16 · *how the Hypocrites, bound in threes, and with transferable heads, strive to shelter behind one another from the arrows / how their triple knots move in this bound struggle / how they are shot / the novice sees G, an acquaintance*

Seeking amidst the terrible swirl and whirl
of analgesic brume, three-tied-together as they were,
as all were, dotted tripping triply the pale expanse,
to not protect each other but themselves from
the pointed punctuations of the air,
the Badly Faithful stuttered back and forth
in fear-retiring fashion, trying each to make cover
of the other. In this way, a countless,
insect horde of tribound deaths
mopped, grovelled, mowed and withdrew,
beating retreats that could not be backwards,
sheltering behind the two that sought themselves
never to be not behind the two that were not them,
ever-changing, exposed, behind,
exposed, behind, exposed, behind,
like a plait of white, slimed hair
without hope from —

oh ouch! ouch! ouch! ouch!

arrows.

Which came in flights, in showers,
flesh-splashing shatters, exploding
breast upon chest upon breast upon chest,
as each was wound unwillingly to the fore.

They fell splat into the whiteness,
bunch-speared: and revived,
quailing from their next destruction,
more fearful of the same agonies.

Surely, I cried, that is G from the Brewery!
No, said Sam, tucking his fawn turtleneck
up upon his chin for the cold white mist,
that is his head. He is there, where he pointed,
with the head of H, and sometimes of I.

They are, you will see,
all wrongheaded.

SONG 17 · *he speaks to the head of G, though it is wounded / he cradles his friend / who tells him that he did not lead by example / the novice is moved / he considers how man might be saved*

I spoke to it while it was down.
I leaned close to it, that is, the noddle.
It seemed foolish to address the bottlewasher's trunklet,
though there was more of it, and though it was he,
for, though it was nearby, it had another's head.

It was a pleasing decision, and Sam agreed to it.

I tiptoed where they lay, all three,
and he, unfortunately for him, in the van,
his sweet head transfixed,
his otherman's body all opened with arrows
and bleeding and broke.

O G, what have you done? I called to his ear,
cradling the corse of H in my arms, attached as it was.
White corpuscles streamed down my bush-shirt.

A Tall Knight damned me, which he wept at.

His tears fell upon his I. I cradled both bits carefully.

I, who danced a furious puha on the beach,
pāua-feathered and afraid,
led dear kin to death   doubted in danger
word-warrior unwilling   by the white-wave sea.

It is a fair moral observation, said Sam,
which will not do him an inkling of good.
Never light so faint as theirs.

But I was sorry.
Can we not learn still too late to be good?
Can knowledge not save us? Repentance not raise?

Not when each day, and each hour
streams like a star into everness.

SONG 18 · *they leave G (with H or I) and have lunch / and continue across the landscape of Wing 3 / they look back upon the carnage / and approach the lift once more*

I laid them gently down all.
The skull-stuck arrows,
helms of thorn-wood,
sharp enquiries, punctuation
seeking reasons both in brains and bollocks.
And tramped away.

Sam and I shared a meringue and a Chinese gooseberry
at the top of a narrow saddle over the pass
to the lift yum. Ascended beyond the mists,
we sucked our spoons on a wet whāriki.
For this was a great, white room,
like its own geography.
For the armies of misdeed were many.

Sam crackled at his small confection,

whose edges flew into fragrant dust on the wind.
And the hairy snack-skins blew away
like little mice
into the wafting world below,
canescent essence of ice.

And below us in confusion they fell,
and fell again before fierce flocks of arrows
flown from goodness knows where,
spouting white blood, and they
squirming back and behind in their squirmy threeknots,
thinking to save what something else thought
was its body, ah,
and climbing back into life
to be torn into shards of belief,
to be risen again.

The wide wide wide wide plain.

So, sadly refreshed, we gained
our battered elevator, and made ready to slide
to a deeper appal.

SONG 19 · *while they wait the lift to Wing 4, the novice asks Mr Beckett how men are judged for their punishment / the guide explains that between the theories of purpose and fatuity we elect the way we live, by which choice we are judged by our own souls / the lift appears correctly*

What is the judge of us, Sam?

The lights on the lift indicated
Up and Down and Arrived.
It was certainly not.
But the rattle, approaching or dying,
seemed from above.

Judge my arse, said Sam, brushing his suit-jacket,

27

and gazing up upon the white shaft,
that boomed like a bullish eructation.

We sat on a Spaniard to wait for the bucket.
Its pricks bled us not.
Sam gazed into the cheese-coloured omneity.

The aether trembles for an instant,
and we are gone. And each immortal maggot
strives upon its purpose, and knows that there is none.
Sam put his stout and failing shoe a little on the black side
upon his knee a little on the worn side,
and continued. I hearkened ever nearer.
Between these dreams that lie
upon the two breadths of a snowflake,
we each alone elect the conduct of our soul:
and by this favour of a breath's length
we ourselves have judged ourselves
by every lost eternal hour
that you may witness now.

The lift screamed Really Arrived
with little tinpot sparks.

Aha! All aboard! cried Sam,
a little smiling on the courtesy
of our machine, which crashed open
upon his last full-stop
with a small burp of burned geranium.

Which did not suit him.

SONG 20 · *a description of the journey to Wing 4 / and of Wing 4 / the power
of descriptive writing / the Exploiters*

    *Clish! Hum. Whoa! Whoosh! Rattle! Whoosh!
Whoosh! Screech! Wobble. Bang! Scrape. Hiss.*

What a fucking interesting journey, said Sam,
as the doors goyled apart.

I stepped out with an innard of some sort
caught
on my hobnails. Ugh.
Had it been from before, or some shredding to come?

I looked out where Sam walked on ahead.
A bloody great staircase leaned into the whitish beyond.
A bloody great red carpet of stains up it.
And all about, the foul fairyness of bubbles.
And at its foot a pale snot-tinted lake
a-twinkle, all a-twinkle in moonlight.

Come, said Sam. I caught a little flappingly
up with him. And we bibbled through
the falling fantastic frothikins. They tickled our extremities.
They biffed and boffed like rubber pearlets
in swirls of zephyrs incarnate.
Bubbly bubbly bubbly bubbles everywhere.

Veils of pale exhausted grapes shook
in worn-electric sud-curtains.

This is the distillation, remarked Sam evenly,
baffing a path amongst the exploding balloonicules,
of longer work.

Do you mean Descriptive Writing? I asked.
Tis the meaning sucked itself from nothing much
in both cases, he replied:
contractions of the damned.

Behold the Exploiters!

We had reached the first filthy red stair.
I agog.

Fondled in a blipping swarm
of merry piss-acid blibs,
these new unshapen creatures slopped and stretched,
howled and hauled upon the staircase.

What are those sacks, so wax-podged and doughy,
so argillaceous, medullary and overripe,
that these loose and kneaded, sad and luckless things
lug and kedge from step to step to squelchy step?

I enquired.

Ha! barked Sam. It is themselves;
the bloodhound flaps of dropsical flesh,
laded with coins of iron, core and gold.

I poppled my way more near.

The carpet squished with trodden phlegm.
I saw a man whose hapless lobes and arsecheeks,
breast and scalp, hung
in dragging loads amidst the moiling muck.
I saw a woman hauling at her own
full-grounded thigh, that thumped from stair to stair
and fetched her over. *Bompf. Bompfitty-bompf.*

Down she goes! roared Sam.
It is a cruel sport, I replied.
They have writ the tune themselves, he said,
whose burden now is only what they won
at need's expense.

It is a cruel sport.

And what do they strain to tearing to grasp
at the top of the stairs, dear Sam?

Some lie of their salvation, I wouldn't wonder,
he replied. And yet I knew he knew I knew he knew,
and that it was.

And will some, I asked,
still in some soft despite of hope,
for I see some far away
upon the stairs amidst the bubbled clouds,
up up there, where the light burns
like hydrochlorics, with little little toils
of strangling bags, come at last
to the last stair of all?

Oh to be sure, said Sam,
and recognise the lie, for it is theirs,
and start upon the next grand climb
upon a pink and gangrened carpet
ripped from the Odeon in Buncrana,
to gain perhaps the inkling of a promise.

And there is J! I cried, upon the fourth!
Oh! Crash! No, upon the third stair.
May I speak with him about his hope?

Be my bloody guest, said Sam.
Only do not stand too long in the burning mucus there,
with your boots of only metal, lace and leather.

Ah, what have you done, dear J? I asked,
dancing upon the third stair like a full bladder.

He had called elves to work in his garden.

He had paid them the price of a pea.
And he sobbed for a pardon.
And wept to be free.

So I squelched away.

And he pulled at his sag-silver scrotum,
that thumped and squeezed at the shagpile.

And I tiptoed back to my guide.

SONG 23 · *they look beyond the staircase, where the Ruthless suffer heart-attacks on a clothesline / the novice retreats in confusion / they make for the lift across the beautiful Plain of Pity*

I looked beyond the awful stairs
where Sam said, There is more.

Strung aloft along oh woe a line of steel
between two tower'd Mt Pylons,
the Ruthless hung on cabled hooks,
aswing from elongated ears,
and crying to the cream unknown.

And now, and now, and now, and now, again,
their stuttered forms in puppet pain
along the long electric string
jangled, heart-attacked and stung
each minute that forever holds
with power,
which perhaps had once been then theirs.

I staggered back against the pantry door.
Who deserves this? I cried.
They who think they do, said Sam.
In all the ages of the world
these million knew the same.

And are there other rooms for other men? I asked.
They are numberless as the judgements of our hearts.
And other wires? I asked again.

I cannot even imagine, I cried,
and slumped to the pus-tiled floor.

Come, said Sam. Cheer up, cheer up,
there is worse to come.

He took me by the arm and led me to
the pretty Plain of Pity, whose
creek-and-kōwhai, mead-meandered shape
proposed it to the sight of all the damned,
to torture them with loss.

Ah, how fair it was, awave with water, pollen all apop,
autumn-russet wheat, cornflowers and Afyon poppies.
I thought of home. They would be picking the hops now.

SONG 24 · *they await the lift to Wing 5 / the novice looks backward / he asks Mr Beckett what place He has been given in judgment / Mr B replies that he will know, for he will be given another guide there*

We waited, I atremble, on a cushion of kānuka.
Sam cleaned his glasses gently on his turtleneck,
with thoughtful circles.
The little flowers twinkled like milk stars,
dreamed with moments of amaranth.

I turned to look back.
The crackled bark and bristles
beneath gave me away.
Sam, dear Sam, did not scold me,
or give me cause to believe his cause.
Even with the tear in my eye.

There, in a vastness of obnubilated pearl,
the ended and eternal world lay all before me.
There, a tiny endless string of hopping silhouettes
like ants expiring jerky in hot cream.
There, the vast busy high red stair
fading into roseate curds.
There the falling eructating pops.
And all about a waste of beauty.

Oh Sam, I said, have *you* come to this?
Sam replaced his blueblind glasses.
This is given you, he said,
because you are not dead.
Happily, I am. Ah, here is the lift.
When we are where I know I shall always be,
I will tell you, and you will know.
There you will leave me thank Christ
for something with a little more diversity of hope.
Get in.

The last swirl of mucilage in the arched sky.
I wiped away my more mere tear.

SONG 25 · *they enter the lift down to Wing 5 / the man in the lift behung with
cats described / Mr Beckett urges the novice to speak to him*

Fuck me sideways! cried Sam, right upon entering the can.
Another bloody bastard stowaway!
Get back, you shit.
He flapped his fingers at its face.

It stumbled into a metal corner.
I looked about for a label.
What was this black-blue creature going up or down?
What was his fair living fur coat,
fairywise or incorruption?

It is there, said Sam with a point.
Stapled to its bloody curtailed genitals.
And it said, 'A Bloody Great Pimp Bastard'.

'Aah!' it cried upon the instant,
for the coat came alive, for fair fur coat it was not,
with an ululation of mewing screech.
And in the lights of vertically passing hell-fires
beyond our little iron grille,
whilst we descended,
I saw him hung with cats,
intoothed and all inclawed,
scrabbling to remove their own sunk fangs
with useless terror,
and skid-blood hindlegs.
And down we went with a swish too,
coloured bright red now and then.

Soon, said Sam, the pussies will stop a moment,
to prolong the novelty of a new attack.
Speak to him while he stands,
in a manner of speaking, before you.

You may call him K for Kunt.

SONG 26 · *the Bloody Great Pimp Bastard / the problem of the continued
destruction of the flesh explained*

O man hooked and cut called Kunt,
I said, tell me why your glory
is long last all gone.

And he told me

That he cruised the streets of Whangerei,
With Annie and Danny and Fanny and Faye,

And whistled sweet as a nightingale,
Pretty lambs for sale!

And the butchers came and bought them there,
And he heard their cries in the evening air,
And he drove away and listened not.
Pretty lambs for the pot!

The lift hurtled flicker-flash down down down,
licked with fires through the iron mesh.
And Sam's clean glasses glittering away
like some bloody heliographic morse gone mad.

And the cats, I whispered. How can they still
have flesh to tear in a thousand years?
Will it not be a flayed and unfeeling bone by then?

There is no worst, it is all the worst.
The quick may never o'ertake the slow,
for when it has reached where the slower was,
the slow has moved, *nolens volens*,
a little on. Ha!

It is thus with the rending of flesh.

And K cried aloud in his tin,
with a terrible Aaaah!

SONG 27 · *they emerge at the suburbs of Wing 5 / a description of the general view /*
they tramp across the shitbog of buried men / to a sign that says Plunderers

Dear God and Jesus Christ to be out
of that pernicious bollocks, said Sam,
as we hurried into a feuillemort sky.
For the cat-coat had started with a start,
like an electric thresher behind us.
The doors clanged, and up he ripped.

Here, said Sam waving generally, live the Abusers,
whose many is necessarily subsectioned,
of the world, ha! if you can call it living.
He peered dully away
at a cataclysm of poisonous, white,
and ginger-rusted towerblocks,
rather worse for wear (the towerblocks),
warping beyond a shit-belching marsh.

It is a pretty hike, but we may stop
and bend our ears upon the way. Come.

We crossed the bog carefully, like Jesus was it
on the Sea of or was it a Lake?
I held hard to Sam's harsh hand.
Had we been fishers of men
we might have made a tidy catch.
But there was no mercy nor pity to spare.

Mouths aflood in stool and chunder
bobbed and went under.
Amber ordure, blood and fluxed,
gushed forth from their voided discomfort beneath,
and slapped up their occluded gasp-holes.
I pinched my desperate nose.
Behold, cried Sam, a sign!
I swung my skull instinctively to the sky.
It was mostly unpleasant.
Have you learned nothing?
There is no salvation here.

And the sign said: Plunderers.
The P and the L were a little unspeakably splattered.
Which made a little joke.

We floated forth.

You may find this hard, little brother,
said Sam, as we ascended the fried concrete stairs
to a claw-shredded door.
For we approach the greater horrors.
But man has made this bloody crux himself,
and are you not a man, and must bear it.

He threw the raddled plank aside.

What may I learn from this? I cried,
throwing my hands before my eyes.

That you cannot go on. That you must go on.

A vast porcelain valley lay all before me,
longer than my unwilling sight could measure,
like some undreamt of Empyrean's bath,
infestedly pullulating with numberless souls
and their match exactly in hogs.
Eaten and chewed in snarled snaps and snatches,
each little Plunderer scrabbled out his agonies
upon the smooth, cool, white, unclimbable
bathsides, seeking ah seeking forever escape,
but sending only their stumped river of gore
into its floor, from where it swirled
in a wave like an almighty's haemorrhage
down a plugole the size of Cork.

The air was a veil of blood,
except that veils are usually
modest and sweet,
modest and sweet.

The quicker.
The slower.
The worst.

Take me away, I cried.
Sam turned at me impatiently.
There is no away, he said.
This is the eternity of one moment.

And what, I demanded,
if one should hate himself
for many things, and many times?
Shall he be here and there in this place?

You may find your alphabet of men again, said Sam,
in universes parallel, tangential, digital,
cardinal, aliquot, reciprocal,
commensurable, incommensurable, logarithmic,
exponential, fluxional, transcendental,
rational and irrational. All of them as ghastly.

And is there no hope, under this deathly sky, I asked.
What can change that is done? said Sam kindly.
This is your mathematic physics, yea,
and your physic mathematics,
not some bloody milk-
and-water bastard
ethological
shite!

Is there a better place,
I cried with trembling lips,
where there is a star to be seen above,
and there is hope to change in the end?

To be sure, said Sam.
We shall come there by and by.

SONG 30 · *they climb to the next door / where the first Abusers are impaled by flora / a woman smells hope upon the novice / the novice comforts her / they move cautiously into the hideous hall*

We climbed to the teetering top.
The foetid penthouses reeled in a wind
of whipping wormwood.
I used my eyelids as a hood.

Ah, said Sam, here we are at Number Twelve.
Knock, friend, and enter.
I performed the first hopelessly as the second
I should say and was invited to the third
by a woman worn by a branch.

There is one among us, she said,
while a series of twigs drove their way
out of her skull, who is not dead.
I can hear the rags of joy
hiding upon his breast
like sunlight, ah sunlight, so long lost
in memories of pain.

Surely it is L, I said, taking her thorny head
into my hands. And she wept that kindness
for a moment softened the bough in her lungs.
That it might hurt the more on its hardening again.
I know what you have done.

We tiptoed to the hall.
Of merry cherry wallpaper and convolvulus linoleum.
A barometer like an eye among wooden leaves.
An umbrella stand of elephant foot.
A lobster telephone.
A dead bracket lamp of fused ideas,
fringed with golden nylon.

Putrid, said Sam.

Along the hall
people come and go.

SONG 31 · *they watch the second Abusers with no minds / and those grown through feed the third Abusers with exploding arms*

Kindness of all kinds forsaking,
Watch them, sweetheart, tormenting
who envy them their pain.

I saw such things as I shall write,
for I am man, and these were once the same.

To feel the need no longer, said Sam,
is a rare deliverance.

These with the ferruginous bathing caps,
he continued, are the men who have lost their minds.
I do not, sure, mean thus mislaid.
I mean they have none.
They have been taken away.
In this eternal, inexistent panic
they have become the instruments of *dies non*.

And these, the floratically impaled,
in the manner of your dear friend L,
would die to be their rose,
their palm,
their olive tree.

And I shall write that here I saw
these remnants of thought and hope
feeding hand-grenades to quailing men,
and reeling in the bloody scraps they made.

We tiptoed back upon the torn limpid splatter-wash
of things divinely made by time,

who once read newspapers, drank milk,
and gave with love gifts at Christmas day.

SONG 32 · *back at the Bog of Shite, they pause for morning tea / the tethered
ghosts described / the novice questions Sam concerning the imagination / he replies
that it cannot save the damned*

And now, thank goodness, adjourned upon an isthmus,
back amongst the Bog of Shite.

Macaroon? said Sam, spreading his handkerchief nicely
across an overkecked mess of mince and mousse.

We gnawed ruminatively. What would I not have guven for a
    lemonade.

I cast my eyes about. The towerblocks reeled.
The purple skies wheeled.
Grey spurts rushed upwards from the city
of the damned, spraying, and fell back.

Hundreds, thousands, millions,
and not one escaped atom there.

Sam, what are they? I asked,
failing and falling ever over the dreadful din?

They are the tethered ghosts, said Sam,
casting his macaroon into an oesophagus
that floated peristalsistically near.

Have we souls then, I asked,
and should we hope despite it all?

Souls? Souls? said Sam. Damn it, child,
they are the pegged minds of men,
seeking separation from their awful duty

in the skies of fancy.
But they will not get away.

Can we not then even imagine our escapes,
when we can conceive such torments?
It was a quiet question.

Flight is in vain, said Sam pityingly.
Beyond, ah, far beyond it will come,
because you think it might,
but not they, not they.

Evolution's pigs.

SONG 33 · *they wait for the lift for Wing 6 / the novice asks if he will bear the*
terrors to come / a riddle game / what the terrors are where they are bound

We reclined having eaten on our elbows eventually
at the shaft, and hearkened to it coming,
boom boom boom boom boom boom.
Sam idly picked the black velvet daisies
that whispered in a velvety way in its leveche.

Can I bear more? I asked him softly.
Ah, said Sam, playing with a panting panicle,
we are done here now
with the old vernacular biting and ripping.
And the screaming, I enquired,
and the gnashing of teeth?
Oh of course them as well to be sure, he said.

I sat up from the lamenting lawn.
What could be more awful? I asked tremblingly.
Ah, imagine, he said.

Shall we play at a riddle. Sam sat up also
from the lamenting lawn, at hands with a pansy.

The lift was apparently busy elsewhere.
At least the button still said UP, as well as DOWN,
and also ARRIVED AGAIN.

What is and is not? said Sam with an academic smile.
Where have we been and must go?
What do we not believe in but know to be true?

Death, I replied. That was easy.
And what is worse?
Imagining death.

That, said Sam,
getting up in a tangle of pantcuffs and boots,
is where we are going.

Oh good, I said, as the lift scraped down
at last to us
ironically.

SONG 34 · *they rush in the can down to Wing 6 / here they see the Killers of Life and Imaginings rushing transparent at the eternal edge of death*

We hurtled down at an angle of forty-two and a bit degrees.
Hang on to your drawers! said Sam.

Thus it must be
when one enters the kingdom of the mind.

Sixth Floor, counting downwards of course! cried Sam.
Behold, these Killers! And he flung from the biceps.
Though the doors were not yet open, it was a great gesture.
Though then they schmoozed out. Upon a dreadful silence.

Upon the darkling plain a mighty multitude of men
ran squirming in their vasty voyaging knots.
Each held his two transparent arms

about his black transparent skull,
and rocked like jokes of grief.
Each glass jaw with gums
like indian ink, and teeth acrack with fear.

You will not know,
because you cannot feel,
that they are on the very brim of death
always and knowing that they will be always nailed
into the fixed eternal moment of their deaths.
Frankly, it is not bearable.
Yet they bear it always, like a burden
that they cannot bear.

This is no thing imagined,
it is the very dissolution of existence,
the mind all gone but nearly nearly gone,
teetering in terror upon the last rip and flood
that drags extinction down upon a little light
into forever's nothing. Always. On and on and on.
A sad immortal mortal end.

I dropped thud to my knees.
The glass plastic seethrough throng
swarmed silently at their eternal utmost fright and finish.

SONG 35 · *the novice recognises M and N and tries to speak to them / he is joined
fingerwise to N for one second / he faints*

Ah! There is M! I wept.
For he, who I had loved, his bitumenic brain and jaw
rubbing at his caving
but never caving
cellophane cranium,
roamed in snaked and useless shakings-off
the dying land that never died
as good as dead and wishing so.

And N, surely, from the archery,
who loved the shining Mongolian bow,
his wheat-white beer and Sunday lunch!

Oh my friends! I hurried at the heaving mess
of last but lasting horror's glass stampede.
What ever could you do to earn a place
in this great panic, who were once
amongst blue wallpaper, and the sofa
and the television, with a sausage on a fork?

They will not answer you, said Sam,
putting his hand against my cheek softly.
They look forward to the long black night,
but it will not come though it is but
a fearful finger-breadth away.

But here, near you now, is your friend,
the sorrowed killer N.
Take his finger in yours but for a second,
and you will feel what he will feel forever.

And forth I flew to the pellucid man.
A little waltz perhaps for old times' sake! cried Sam.
Two! Three!
And thus we touched.

And I fainted upon an instant at the touch:
You will be gone forever.
You will not exist, eternally.
You will fucking die.

SONG 36 · *the novice wakes to a vision of hope / Sam explains from whence it has come*

And I saw, in a golden bubble,
amidst this great dark plastic silence,
most of the men who had ever lived

under a white tree,
and yellowglass pears on it,
in a day of moderate sunshine,
a kind of Pakawau springtime,
and hardly in much of a hurry
to do anything
but be sunshined
and, well, amongst.

And the bubble stayed,
a little flattened where it sat,
and then bounced gently,
to the gentle amusement
of the field of gentlefolk within,
and bounced a little higher every time,
like an arseabout progress of earth-bouncing,
and burbled bobblingly into the darkness,
gleaming away like a slumber-heavy cat's-eye.

Hm. This has come, said Sam, a little shortly,
from a day once upon a time
that you passed, if the hour returns to you rightly,
with dear M and darling N himself,
upon a fair furlong of lawn and daisies,
where you shot the varnished bow, ah!
to be followed hard upon by Sunday lunch,
with any amount of wheat-white beer,
and a sausage with blue wallpaper
on a television with a fork in a sofa
or some such sweet contented bollocks.
Which is to say
that man may be damned in a moment,
though he be fat and fair forever else.

I lay a little on my back more,
and watched the upside-down men
with glass heads winding by
on silent screams and cracking teeth.

And now where we will go,
to the most dreadful,
is a long way down.
I have sandwiches for the journey.
Some strenuously bactofuged Weisslacker,
and Ammerländer Schinken,
pink as rosepetals and dewed.

I could not detect his tone.

It is, my dear friend, a crowded land,
and you could not bear it,
ha, I cannot bear it,
who can bear anything?
It is none of it easy,
but that it has to it
the happy life forever in its sight.
For they who yearn in torment there,
their torment is its sight: for you,
for you it is the glaucous passage merely
to a better place, where I will leave you.

Leave me? I asked quietly.
Shall we go? he replied. We began to do it.

O there is O! I fell to my corduroys.
The grey dust bulged
like a cat under a blanket.

O O! I cried. Long use of terror
had ground his skull to sand. He stalked
beseeching something always not to die,
a screaming sack of glass-bound dust
with two popped eyes

convulused like pleached electric wires
black with the odour of shortcircuits.

O O, what did you kill?
And I heard his indian-ink-soaked larynx-beach
weep in waves O not please again not please again.

Again and forever, said Sam.
We will go now.

SONG 38 · *they take the lift to Wing 7 / a jackal-headed companion described /
his label misread haha*

The lift crawled with olivaceous rotted honeysucklestems.
Steam jellied at the metal walls,
questing miasmic at our recoiling apertures
with leatherette glove-probes
anointed with catfood and boiling water.

I made a face.

Imagine that, said Sam. Bonne bouche?
He opened the sandwich-tin.
With an alpine scene.
Which suddenly clished to the floor.

Holy Mother of Jesus God! said Sam.
Fuck me in the Folterzimmer!
What is that?

Ein *etwas* emerged from the hot, percolated stench.
A small white skirty and sandals,
succeeded by the handsome breast of a warm brown land,
and a tremendously ridiculous cardboard head-creation
with salient ears and aureated eye-oles,
all in the likeness of a er …

Doggy?

The label! The label!
In the name of all the bloody angels!
cried Sam, recovering the Samnaun Alps.

It says, I exclaimed,
fumbling with the little beige cardboard
in the difficult optical conditions,
that he is A Nudist.

Bugger me, said Sam, eyeing the creature,
is this now a fresh sin?

SONG 39 · *they shoo the creature to its corner / cheese and ham sandwiches described*

Get back, get back, you foul and frantic misconception!
Sam advanced upon it, threatening
with the blue sky of a May Swiss afternoon.

A small wet flash
gathered moistly in one eyehole.
Is there a head in there? I said,
flapping my beanie at its nutty nipples.

It retreated sensibly, one bronzed hand
against the Hexenkopf.

There is sand on its sandals, I said.
What else should there be, said Sam.
It darkled back to its kettle.

It was hard in the circumstances
to enjoy properly
our cheese and ham sandwiches,
knowing that a great sinner
crouched in the putrid dank of dark and steam nearby,

whilst we hurtled, not quite plumb,
at a hundred miles an hour
towards the ultimate perturbation.
But we did well enough.

The cheese rind was especially saporous.
The ham on the whole maybe a little emulsive.
What wouldn't I give now, said Sam with a sigh,
for a nice jewfish caught from the dear bridge
at Ballina.

We threw bits of buttered breadcrust to the dog.
They were unyielding.

SONG 40 · *the gigantic lounge of Wing 7 and the False Gods described / the novice wonders at the deportment of its inhabitants / and is answered by Sam*

Were you ever at LAX?

The liftdoors pinged open and we stepped out
arm in arm beneath their shitted yellow arrow
blinking in a custard box of frosted glass
that muttered with scorched dead bits of huhubugs,
the arrow not us.

The Nudist glided softly out behind us to his doom
like a hovercraft.

Was this what I could not bear?

About a soiled avocado carpet ten miles long
drifted the False Gods. They reclined and chatted
upon olive plastic sofas, drinking cocktails
clear and oily, and eating cheerios on toothpicks.

Upon a monstrous plastic kitchen table
draped in a cheerfully tartaned latex blanket,

stood a gigantic wooden hedgehog
quilled with a million little cocktail sticks
of pineapple cubes, corned beef squares,
baby tomatoes, glacéd fruit, processed cheese,
fishmould and mushrooms, peppers of all kinds,
diced pork, pickled gherkins and stewcubes.
It grinned with two buck teeth the size of fridges.

Lit by merciless neon strips
the dead ones circulated, smoking, chatting,
drinking and nibbling.
The sound of throttled laughter
wirbled around a thousand chromium standard lamps.

I wonder at their deportment, I said.
You have guessed I think, said Sam close to a wall,
that we are watching the damnation of hearts and minds.

SONG 41 · *the novice looks about the vasty crowd and mingles / his guide expatiates upon the bearing of the damned*

Take a galette, said Sam, heigh-ho,
and perhaps an oil Martini,
light up and mingle!

I approached the hedgehog,
and plucked out a fisheye-and-strawberry-jam gobbet.
I lit a cigarette and balanced a Babycham
upon the edge of a plastic stereogram.

Good morning, if that is what it is,
I addressed a passing himation.

He turned his rheumy eyes upon me,
and sniffed at my mortality
with a kind of longing fear,
and fled.

52

I plunged amongst the party dresses.

You will notice, said Sam, pressing on behind me
with a small live crustacean on a needle,
the venerable intent,
the significant eye,
the philosophic air,
the pedagogic mien,
the triumphant djellaba,
the humilious beaver,
the ineffable tread,
the compassionate glare ...

He paused to swallow his panting morsel.

Indeed I had seen them all,
who were thus.

And guess perhaps?

SONG 42 · *Sam explains who are the damned / the novice enquires as to the*
possible necessity of gods / the guide pooh-poohs divinity / and mingling halts

We sat on a pinkplush stool
at a vasty rank of Hammond organs.
I put my glass on the varnish,
which melted in prismatic terror.

These are the mighty fallen, said Sam,
taking a massicot sip,
who spurned the truthful mess of man
to posit damned divinity;
who gave no reason more for hope
than the advancement of their own content;
who —

Can that be — ?

Ah, said Sam, a little moist about the eyeballs,
all our dear damned lords and saints,
and all theirs too,
that we have seen in books
or never known.

P and Q and R and S, that I had seen
in pictures and in prayers.

And are they not, I asked,
as robed and barefoot sages swept
their martyred and transfigured wounds
across the pretty party swill,
waiting on apotheosis and the light
that will not come, the necessary flesh
that clothes our desperate dreams?

Pooh, said Sam, at his own strength,
old earth, no more lies.

I ceased to mingle,
hemmed on all sides
by whisp'ring cardboard, tinsel, sellotape and glue,
how the heads and wings of all divinity are made.

SONG 43 · *the novice wonders about their punishment / Mr B explains / the Great Black Blind rises terribly*

How do they suffer? I asked.
Intermittently, said Sam. But exquisite. Ah,
in fatal jealousy and disillusion in their peace,
and dreadful envy and despair
upon the raising of the Great Black Blind.

This made each particular hair about my arse
stand on end like quills upon the fretful porcupine.

The Grate Block Blonde? I stuttered.
And is it here?

Behold, said Sam. It was of old his favourite word
for drama, and this surely was.

Glasses shattered to the stinking carpet.
Canapes slithered amongst sandals.
Cigarettes as well as mine
tumbled turning fire down the air.
A general oozing gasp.

And the Grape Blick Blend began to raise
with an oiled hissssss.

This is hourly forever, said Sam helpfully.
And the other eternal half of eternity.

A thousand miles of western wallblind rose,
unrumblingly and slow,
letting in a golden light
and the sound of bagpipes
upon the lying souls,
all transfixed
where blooded wounds filled
their foreheads, hands and feet and breasts,
impaled upon their gored and terrible attention.

What comes? I turned to Sam, his lit face.
It is worth seeing, he smiled.

SONG 44 · *the False Gods tormented by life from which they are forever excluded*
as they did unto it / a description of the other side of the Great Bluck Blind

Still it wound slow slow upwards,
the whole world's safety curtain,
bleck and blint.

And there we set the scene:

the whole front faces of the godmeant damned,
like tourists at a Tioman sunset,
burning more more higher higher
gilded angel-bright and horrorstruck,
and dark and cold behind;

Behold! cried Sam again, a little feared I thought,
the world that they have lost
for their deluded braver sky
that never was
but in the slothful death of their courage
to bear the life that cannot be borne
that is all ours!

and there in early sunset's Schubert-glow
the honking merriment of man,
whose bright resigned mechanick work today was done,
and now to be together only
was his verray bliss;

the moderately happy undeceived
about their pleasure,
that fired the fronts of falsest faith
and ripped their bloody hearts with rue.

SONG 45 · *more of the vision of the moderately happy undeceived / more of the tortures of the false gods and their prophets / they are all so, that is, false*

More of this:

the golden view,
the ruminant-autumnal-merry-wayzgoose-time,

where folks in smocks and beanies
bouncing brave on common benches

stuffed their faces full
with pancakes, pizzas, popcorn, peasey-pudding,
parsnips, port and pop,
and singing Little Titch and Sweet Maid Nut,
and dancing hiphophip
in codpiece-placket fat vicinity
to the howl of bagpipe bands,
and others in their windows red and chortled
entered from behind by half-lit happy bumpkins,
where the village trees waved gilded branches at their junket,
and far away the purple hills of heather glowed
with all that we could well expect
from this brief simple life.

And more of them:

whose jealous selves unseen
and gambled on the dice of endless dark,
tore like heavy zips in bodybags
and left the flesh they had forsook
in party dress and heavens' hopes
still staring gormless ghastly and
injected with regret like bad cocaine.

See how they shake, said Sam,
and at the best,
brief losses of consciousness.

Come now, he said, taking my tartan fuzzy sleeve,
it is time to leave this all.

And where do the gods go that are good? I asked.
There is no other adjective but these, said Sam.

Q. And is there no Best Bastard of the World
    torn limb from limb forever as example
    to everything that ever lived and lives?
    Some centre to this endless sink of souls?
    Some unimagined spot where something foul
    gives illustration of the worst of man?

A. This is not a literary exercise, dear child,
    this is time and truth according to
    the laws of time and truth; an observation
    of unalterable acts and their sad ends
    that have already happened, and cannot be made-up
    to dance upon a limelit stage
    for silly examplets in a player's course,
    or speech
    to teach
    or preach.

Q. Where shall we go now,
    having seen all and the worst?

A. We shall go to a Better Place.
    Soon, if you keep your eye succinctly
    upon the far horizon there beyond the drinks cabinet,
    a Quite Good Man will appear in showers of silver foil
    bearing an elasticatible Klein Bottle
    about which we will whizz upon our arses
    to an Elsewhere with no boundary with this
    while yet within it or without
    of which there is neither.

Q. Struth.

A. Himself.

We passed the trembling tinkle of the cabinet,
its spectral fear pressed like sparkling knives against
the liver plastic handles from within.

I took one momentary glimpse
of its light-shouldered doors,
a sheeted pane of its ajar-shaped golden moment
cut out
and then gone.

And there wept T, at the backside,
where the cheap cardy plywood
hammered on with minor nails
showed its unconnected face.

And is that U? O
U, who led the faithful
to the fountain and the dingled ram
upon the very night of someone's war,
and blew its horns?
Who now, without the memory of life,
stared upon the copper cabinet foot
to find the man that made it
in some dream.

We crossed the concrete patio,
and a celibate orchard of plums.

And came next to the breast of a mighty hill,
whose slope declined before our feet
a thousand miles
of polished alabaster slide
towards some sudden sunnish end.

Sam removed his hat,
and took my hand to the edge of the helter.

Hold onto yer privates, he said.

And out we stepped.

SONG 48 · *the ecstatic slide and what they saw in the sky as they wheeeeeed*

His was a gnarly skin.
But I had come to love him more than anything
and meant not to let my Sam go.
I cannot speak for his own opinion of myself,
yet he seemed to hold a little pressure
about my hand too, perhaps with some small version
of my own feeling and intent.

Wheeeeeeeeeeeeeeeeeeeeeeeeeeeeeeeeeeeeeee!
We were off.

I have never known such peace.
No winds disturbed my generous ears,
no slipstreams my beanie.
We simply silent sped,
digitally decussed,
in aeronautic ecstasy,
chuted down our slick glissade,
now and then executing,
with no intent or ado,
a polished rotation,
the gyring pirouette of champions.

I looked up to the lightening skies,
and, proceeding with quiet quickness,
observed V, W, X, Y and Z,
disposed on high as twinkling points
upon a pentagonic star,

seated each in an Alvar Aalto laminated chair,
one green, one red, one yellow, one blue and one white,
enwrapped in silver cloaks
upon the silver air.

Look! I said circularly to dear Sam,
our glances passing complementary as planets
while we swept onwards downwards,
there is V, and W, with X and Y. O, and Z!
How is it with them?

I waited for my answer
in a hundred miles an hour of silence.

SONG 49 · *Sam explains, at top speed, how it is with V, W, X, Y and Z / what happens at the end of The Bad Place / some small matter of physics*

Ah, they are dj-dj-djust dj-dj-djudged,
said Sam, his cheeks flapping with velocity,
and off to dj-dj-djoin the djdjdj-djdj-djoylflflflful!

And the star, streaming in our direction too,
lit and furnished like a stageful of scenery,
waved at us.

Why do they lie so close
to the lost and the lucky at once? I asked,
turning gently with Sam on my arm.
Was there some doubt of them?

They stood upon a knife's edge;
but their weakness was softened by knowledge,
their fault by a better intent,
their sin by a saviour within.

I waved back.

Sam unfolded to the little more horizontal,
and we picked up speed.
The star cranked itself with us
towards the bright lemon edge.

Whoooooosh!

And we left the place,
shooting off its polished rump
into a kind of sequestered dawniness.

Where we hung. Or fell.

And here, said Sam, over the horizon
comes our Quite Good Man himself
to collect us with his darling Klein Bottle,
and take us to a Better Place
via an indescribable Vorhandenheit of cosmogony.

SONG 50 · *how they enter the Klein Bottle / and pass to the environs of The Better Place*

In a gorgeous sky-wide shower of silver foil,
little falling bits and glistering ribbons,
the Quite Good Man swam at us
through his light-yellow immateriality,
past multitudes of dancing stars,
like a swan upon sparkly wavelets,
bearing in his arms a great floppy item
that appeared, now and then,
to resemble a pair of copulating wineflagons
that shared, from great love, a body and a soul.

To this we were joyfully sucked,
and, in a flash, popped within.

For a moment only, as I passed,
I saw His great bright ski-hat

and parka of singing constellations,
his galactic waterproofs and meteoric boots,
his ginger Kelly beard aflowin,
before I wound, feet first,
with Sam still adorably at hand,
into the rosy-elastic flowermouth of his Bottle.
Or jug.

Here we bounced upon a moisty,
honey-blushing embouchere
of nectared flesh,
both within, thus glimpsing the approaching dawn
in all its lemon-and-limeyness,
and without, in womby pinkness,
from innerlight to outerlight and neither,
and both of them joy.

I believe that this was hope,
the elementary condition
in which we were poured
perpetually
into The Better Place.

II

THE BETTER PLACE

II

THE BETTER PLACE

SONG 51 · *in which there is a short getting used to the new surroundings / and a sign*

Which did not suit so well my Sam,
though I feared now that I would lose him
to his element.

We were laboured out onto a spring lawn,
whence Man and Bottle faded upwards
in a shiver of silver,
and something like a song hummed.

Hum, said my present guide,
settling his billycock from the bump.
We sat on the lawn in a glad-green silence,
and looked about us with our toastie-pies,
and a kind of cautious pleasure.
For we feared now nothing more of carnal assault,
and were surrounded quietly by the opposite of ambush.

We crunched easily, and a happy animal squealed.

What is hope here, I asked dear Sam,
for I saw it, though perhaps only in these silvers and greens,
and a middling manner of sunshine,
and a burbling merriment of water,
and a restorative of flowers
around me, though I had not looked at my back.

It is a bourgeois enema, said Sam.
He threw his black crusts amongst the bibbling daisies.
I am not sure how long I can stand it.

So I looked at my back,
for I did not like eggies much.

There was a small signpost.
It said, 'To Rest is Not to Conquer'.
Its foot was planted in a little fountain of baby toetoe.

SONG 52 · *they climb a heathery knoll together / and gain a whole view of The Better Place / which is a tree, and generally described*

We wandered then by a mossy path
to a purple knoll, swishing and swoshing
through a feathery heathery,
soft and luminous with bubbled buds.
We climbed the hillock circuitously,
which begot a slow-motion dizziness
that wound from our hatted heads
into the pearl-grey air.

The top was bald.
Decoratively speaking.
Except for.
We put our necks up and gaped.

Jesus, said Sam. But it was, in actual factual,
a mighty, mighty tree.

Picture if you can a mighty, mighty tree,
a tree so mighty that it would wake you
with wonder from a dream.
And that is what it *was*:
and not, for dreams or poetics, *like*.
Probably a permutation of pine, said Sam,
goggle-gobbed, even he.

Clear to the top, several miles through the air,
it tapered taperingly in its flocculent greenness;

and upon its last luminous leaf there something danced aglitter,
tiny as an atom, and happy as a midge
turned into diamond.

The whole gigantic creakery murmured in its stillness,
with a murmur of movement and no sound.

We lowered our breathtaking faces,
and our numb-cricked necks,
across which palmed sweet caraway air.
But I could not help but look up again soon,
and this time without Sam,
who was not so easily its friend.

SONG 53 · *the auratic atmosphere about the mighty tree / the leafy transports / the
hopeful commuters / the happy password / the way up / all described*

I recognised in the winding air
an *aura* of tree; exactly of the mighty tree it was,
though outside it, like a glaucous circumjacency,
or a faerie tea-cosy set upon it.

Within the slow, enchanted whirl of this,
leaves like flying carpets came and went,
about and about, and ever upwards,
rocking folks from branch to higher branch:
and they, on this anabatic pleasure-cruise,
seemed from mouthing mouths to be chatting excited,
their little legs swingling over the leafedges,
their little shoes near dancing in the ever-leaving lower air,
and a gondoliering deer, or rabbit, or glistening tuatara
poled them up and on, conquering, I suppose.

And now and then some got off.
And some were collected.
And some stayed for another ride.
And some cried silently ooh and aah.

I turned to Sam.
He was staring at the bald beauty of the dust-drenched,
root-rumpled, grain-gold ground.
I hope, I began.
Aha! cried Sam, looking up immediately
with a satisfied snarl.
I could not say it.
Now we are free to shuffle on.

The dear man seemed to know
that we would thus begin to,
and, to be sure, a large leaf drifted swiftly out
from the tremendously lowermost branches,
driven by a Pukeko.

It spiralled down at us and landed with a pffft.
The Pukeko sported a fez.
Branch line haha, it said.
Trunk line to Bower 1 haha, it said.
All aboard.

We stepped onto the rocking green gloss.

SONG 54 · *the journey up to Bower 1 / the trunk staircase considered / some moments of pleasure / the novice makes an initial tentative lunge at the nature of hope and salvation*

In its endless early afternoon
we screwed serenely up and up
through the soft taupe-and-verdant cocoon.

Our pilot, though silent, plied his pole with pleasant pride.
We glided first around the trunk,
which might hold up the world with its mighty pillar.
A small wood-winged stair wound around it
from the great gold ground at its foot
to the shades of the lowest branches.

I asked Sam what use it was,
but he could not bring himself to be kind.
I think the Pukeko was perhaps the last straw.
Maybe, I thought, it was a way for the fallen,
for fallen there must be, what from the branches, twigs,
aeronautic leaves and continuous passages requiring balance and
    order,
to get back to this Place after a plummet or two,
and begin again the jolly journey up.

I hummed to the boatlike rock of our upping.
I smiled at other passing crafts.
I waved at their passengers.
I gazed in wonder at the tree.
I bathed in the temperate air.
I looked forward to our better adventure.

Glorious prospect, said Sam.
But do not be transported by hope.

Do you mean, I said,
speaking away from the Pukeko for fear of a pun,
that this is only a kind of dream.

Ah no no, it is real enough, replied my best guide,
tapping his ash beyond the leaf-veins and into the warm grey,
though salvation may be only a thought in the making.

Bough 1, Bower 1, said the Pukeko bowing,
and we landed with a poff on a little twig pier.

SONG 55 · *questions questions questions / a Better theory of time and morals
explained, part 1*

Enchanting little fucking woodland creature, said Sam.

It punted away on its shining leaf,

whose bow made gentle splashes in the pearly oxygen
as it clove forwards and down.

We collected ourselves,
for I did not know what to expect,
or how eternity had chosen its hopeful
or arranged its saved.

So I said, What is in this Bower, dear Sam,
and why can the damned not climb here ever
while the saved may mountaineer and mariplane
amongst the branches in betterment,
and how are the hopeful described,
and why have the saved passage always upwards,
and how is expectation possible,
for where we have been burned in the vacuum
of captured time, and mere repetition,
and had no change,
and is this what hope is? (?????)

Jesus wept, said Sam,
as we walked along a branch
wide as the Waikato flow.
Here are all of your answers themselves:

Although we shall behold again, within this mighty tree,
the moment of fault held hedged to itself unending
amongst the multitudinous mathematical series
of measurable and immeasurable moments
about our brief and little clutter of limbs and organs,
the pilgrims of this place may labour hopefully
because —

Hallooo! cooed the Pukeko, passing nearby
with a new leaffull of eager faces that smiled on us.

I have lost my bloody thread.

A pinecone thundered silently past
like a frilled and misericordian meteorite.
Where was I, said Sam.
May labour in hope because, I said.

Ah yes. May labour in hope because –
this was something of a book,
and not a thesis grown of a natural joy for my dear Sam –
upon that dim *un*fatal moment of their sin,
an *aura*, battened and jointed upon it,
the individual and divisible representation
of this pile of mystic bosky snot glowing here in our bloody faces
at every bloody turn about this bloody tree,
a kind of verdant tea-cosy of apprehended remorse or sorry knowledge
of a kind of visceral and intellectual falling off from something better,
which better remained present do you see
from the knowledge of a falling off from it,
without which no falling off might be perceived,
though it might well have occurred,
ah –

Here, Sam and I paused upon Bough 1
to let a gigantic Wētā clatter by upside down along the bark,
kicking its thorny hinder legs like a Lipizzaner,
and a long blue balloon in its slender antennae.

There is a party somewhere, said Sam.
Where was I.

Though it might well have occurred, I said.
That is a general bastard of a sentence, said Sam.
And the thread of it is snapped
by that ugly fucking insect.

We waited amidst the soft helter-skelter of frondescence.

But Sam drove his verbal carriage forth at a froth,
with all the clatter of a just-wound clock
rushing in the Limerick landaulet.

Which I summarise here below:

the *aura* already mentioned, present here about the mighty tree,
and, as I understood it, in a smaller but representative version
about the actual falling-off, I mean its very moment,
which, in the case of the happy folk here,
unlike the miserable shites quote there we had seen Below,
could thus be termed *un*fatal, as Sam had indeed termed it,
emanated from the apprehension of some Ideal
contemporaneous upon that moment,
whether particular to that moment,
or generally held and operative therefore then.

Which was mostly the nub of it so far, I think.

This Ideal, then, in the matter of words,
manners, actions, deeds, conduct, policy
and so forth, accorded with
the apprehension of failure, or falling-off for which
the moderate sinners of this Place had indeed gained this Place,
and by which, and the operation of which,
they had not concluded amidst the unshiftable horrors
exercised upon the miserable shites quote below for all eternity.

Consider the ladder, said Sam,
consider the upwards motion,
always the upwards motion.
And here he waved his arms, revolvingly upwards,
towards the vastness of mighty treetop,
whilst I considered the ladder and the motion.

Now this apprehension, (I am to the precis once more)
is itself, of course, a dimension, which dimension,
moral in its very actual construction,
may be preceived as a kind of tunnel, tube, cylinder,
adjutage, subway, underpass, adit, qanat or sewer,
or at the same time alternatively and concurrently
a globe or world running at an obtuse angle
to the planet wherein the fault itself
is caught in its eternity itself
(as we had observed already unalterably below)
permitting passage, method, pass, way, road etcetera
towards that Better Place, this where we are,
added Sam helpfully, with a panoramic nod,
which may exist, possibly exist, upon it,
or with it or because or instead of it possibly,
that may be followed itself pursued itself or looked for itself,
being as it is or was or will be
part or alternative or branch indeed
from that fault itself again as before
and now and forever.

Here, a Horse-Stinger buzzed by,
wearing a billycock much like my Sam's,
though with a more domestic air.

But the B. horses were sure agallop,
and I was astride, and in for the ride all.

Thus these happy folk may see (in my shortness), recognise or conjure,
it being contemporaneously a part of their original fault,
that part of the fault that led or leads from the fault
to the possibility or presence of betterment,
and thus therefore so here in this blasted tree
they may affix themselves once more to their better selves,
upon a branch or bough or branch or twig or indeed leaf,

always upwards always ever upwards tending,
and thus gaining in the end the Good end which sparkles thus aloft
which was after all and all considering and all together
a part section or adjunct of their possibility even in fault
which has been preserved as an accessible alternative
and can be grasped as damned interruption and smiling prove.
So will that do.

SONG 59 · *concerning morality / the Puriri Moth / Sam exclaims upon the dear dark earth*

I had followed all this with all my best intention.
The lovely shiny grey air helped I think.

Our tittup concluded at the next corner.

And thus, my friend, *morality,* said Sam, grabbing at the reins,
though it have the stench of the collared man about it,
is your man in the physics and the time.

Now here I believe that Sam had,
to his own considerable mind, done his race,
for he proceeded along the barky bough
towards a sweet little round painted door and leaded windows
ahead of us in the tree's trunk.

And I followed. As I had.

A Puriri Moth swirled gently upwards
upon a wave of warm, silvery air,
its spotted extremities like happy eyes
that dwelt only upon hope.

And Sam said,
What decency holds still unextinguished in the affairs of men
is shared with the dust of the earth, the mud of it,
and the loam, the dear dead earth that bears us, ah,

for a moment perhaps in this little light.

He became a little light,
and hurried towards the windows.
I think there is a little light
in my worse moments, he said.
Though I did not catch this particular bus,
for all I desired was darkness.
Yet it runs upon its time
between the each requested stops
of dark and dawn.

SONG 60 · *they enter Bower 1, containing The Selfish / the nature of it / they go out upon a little bridge to view the scene below*

And to answer your last damned question,
said Sam, knocking at the left little diamond-leaded window
let into the boley trunk, what is here
are The Selfish so.

Which was the answer I desired most,
the rest of it being fol-de-rol.

The little window opened by a latchet,
and we struggled through it one by one,
while Sam's glasses fell off.

Within was a furious-full fumous cylinder
about the size of Oamaru,
which we were now within.
If there were a ceiling, or top, it was bloody smoked away.
There was certainly a floor, or bottom.
For there were things there that flew not, and floated not.
Though that was all mostly darkness.
And the rest was bark. That is, the long inside.
As if we had been one moment viewing a dizzy pine,
which had, the next, turned inside-out.

Flomp.

Sam led us out upon a little wooden bridge,
restoring his eyepiece.
The sort that mad young lovers hurl themselves from
in Swiss alpine village stories.
The bridge, that is.
A linsey-woolsey of latticed loglings.

We ventured to its gentle-arching middle.
Let us look up first, said Sam.
So first we looked up.

SONG 61 · *looking up in Bower 1 / the exhaust fumes / the guardian Titiwai /
their mysterious lights*

Liver, ash, madder, brimstone and smalt
were the shades of the flatus:
they swam in the top of the tube
in horror of their own melding.

Neither substance nor commodity,
they tumbled without purpose,
angered and sorrowful,
within their own detrition,
rising used, expiring unwanted,
gathering unhelpful and living unloved.

And in them, through them,
stitching and darting and floating
like diamonds aglitter,
purposed and calm,
the guardian Titiwai busied
about some business
that I could not guess.

Their phosphorescent arses,

red, green and orange,
described in lovely curlicues
the method of their industry.

What are they about, I asked Sam,
in whose lenses the little perfect fireworks
swooped and bibbled
between here and there.

Let us look down now, said Sam.
So now we looked down.

SONG 62 · *looking down in Bower 1 / The Selfish in their bloody-tensioned traffic*
jam

And there below, locked fast
in their discontinued models,
sat men and women with no company,
each in its driver's seat, and not driving.

They stared straight ahead
in agonies of untempered stress,
while the cars, grey, orange, ochre, tan and khaki,
blistered with rust-sores
that blossomed slow as the making of rocks.

Bumper to bumper,
wing to wing,
door to door,
in a great road of a hundred thousand lanes,
they juddered and leaked,
waiting for the lights to change.

And each moment, you see, said Sam,
a terrible expectation of release.

And will they not be released, I said.
All in good time, said Sam.

All in good time.

And the miasma of slag rose
all sooted from a million pipes.
And they stared through their windscreens,
clawing their steeringwheels,
tearing unseen at their upholstery,
and bursting their horns and their hearts.

SONG 63 · *the novice recognises the driver of a Hillman Avenger / he is taken
down amongst the traffic by the Titwai / he hears the song of a selfish woman / and
sees her desperate self*

Surely that is Eh! I cried,
looking down through the mozzy-splashed windscreen
of a festering Hillman Avenger.

Ha! said Sam, She is singing.
Go down and hear her tralala.

How shall I descend?

Leap from the fucking woodwork.

I clambered upon the rustic balustrade.
Whereupon I heard a lovely coo
commingled with soft luminescence.

That there could be such beauty amidst fetor!

A hundred Titiwai fell,
like the shower of a Roman Candle,
down upon my shoulders, and,
taking my tramping shirt in their tiny legs,
each that shone like a long, perfect sentence,
bore me downwards to the rusted rooves and bonnets,
their smoky wings, veined with caramel,

buzzing with a tune I thought I knew.

I put my face to the old curved glass.
And my palm, like at the pictures.
I could hear the song of Eh, faintly from her metal cell.

She sang of a road that was clear,
and sped through a country of green grass,
and trees with tops like giant pompoms,
surpassing the passengers of her life,
and its companions, for her smile.

And for a moment she turned her face to mine,
and her palm, like at the same picture, to mine,
and her tears, and her mouth like a nailed black box,
punished and saved.

I hovered backwards up twinklingly.

SONG 64 · *a strange and infrequent moment in the traffic jam / and a minuscule movement / the echo of Eh*

The Titiwai dropped me softly back on the bridge.

I think, said Sam, we are about to witness a monstrous wonder.
I feel it in my water.
How is that, I said.
Seventeen years ago, he smiled sadly,
running his gnarly finger about his turtlenecked neck
between the knitting and the skin,
a traffic light some hundred miles down the road
turned green for the smaller part of a second:
behold!

I saw that Sam had regained a little of his form,
and stared carefully into the hideous press below.

Suddenly, the million motors revved
with a bilious eructation of liverish smog,
gears crashed, the drivers, their hearts attacked,
their blood apump, clutched their steering-wheels,
and howled towards their salvation
one half an inch, re-nerved, tormented and jangled.

And fell back amongst the leatherette once more,
to wait and wait in electric anguish and expectation.

I saw Eh mouthing her little echo of hopeless hope
through her fouled windscreen:
Upon the open road I sing
And something something something Spring
And bring me something there at last
When all is something something passed.

That will not be soon, said Sam.

SONG 65 · *the mysterious lights of the Titwai revealed / the novice and his guide
leave Bower 1*

We clottered back along the Swissy bridge.
Sam lit a cigarette.

The Titiwai danced around our hats.
What with the talk of traffic and such,
I enquired of smoky Sam, have *they* any part,
being red, orange and green in their hinder lights,
in the tardigrade mechanism of forgiveness?

They are the moral reflection of belief, said Sam.
Which I could not understand,
each word being too much of the abstract to be borne.
And additionally the impulse,
informed by the previous,
of the far lights of permission.

This I nearly got, though not how,
which I did not press, as I did not need it really.

As apes type out the Ayenbite of Inwyt, said Sam,
the greens, the oranges and the reds
may fly momentarily into a disposition
of matching hues all; and the lights will change.

Ah, I thought was enough.
So, said Sam.

We pushed and pulled each other
creasingly through the little leaded window.
Sam kept his glasses close.

Now, he said, we shall wait
for the next fucking foliole.

SONG 66 · *the winsome Weka / the journey up to Bower 2 / a conversation
with Bee and Cee / a small consideration of prayers / all continue up*

This was punted by a winsome Weka.
Baa 2! it screamed.
Wearing a Peruvian cloche
with motley dangly bobbles.
Gawain arp!

Sam lowered the sunglass extension to his spectacles.
Tiggy Winkle, he said,
and fell into a dead cut.

And arp arp we went,
the turquoisey opalescence of the voyaging leaf
billowing gently like a happy lilo
beneath our bums.

As Sam sat apart, I joined the new deliveries

in their pleasantly crowded petiole,
wagging my legs also in the diaphanous air
upon the edge of its fragrant deck.

You are not of the captured and caught,
said one, who was transparently Bee.
You have the texture of one untaken.
A kind of soapy savour, said Cee.
I could not help but notice that they each
had a small Keha drinking at their breasts,
like a hunting brooch pinned in skin.

Truly, I said, I am Just Visiting.
What shall I see ahead?

Ah, here they did a little plainsong together:
More than fleas,
More than these,
Pray for us please.

I said I would, half-believing now
that moral vibes and spiritual requests
might set the aura of the mighty tree
atremble in the slightest.

Up through which we sailed,
impelled by the winsome Weka.

SONG 67 · *they crawl into Bower 2 / where they find a great reading lecture / the Floating Beardo described / and his interminable holy message / the student Fauna-flouters listen in utmost boredom*

While Bee and Cee enjoyed their last green light
upon the branch at a general picnic,
soon to follow us, but for near forever,
and the Weka wurbled away,
Sam and I crawled through a gate of bracken-brush,

and were delivered brushily into Bower 2.

A heavy oaken tablet hovered
in the centre of the slightly sprouty cylinder.
At it grasped a little undulating papery-crumply Beardo,
in a snot-soiled nightshirt and curling-wig,
turning interminably with his little fingers,
tippy-toesywise,
the pages of a bloody great book,
and droning his interminable bloody vapouring,
on and on and on and on and on and on and on
via his tedious-toucan nose.

The whole yaaaaawning caboodle revolved gently,
addressing itself in turn
to his beaten-bored students at all degrees,
and the piece of the matter of the moment
that we came to was:

mostly concerning the fowl of the air,
and the fishes of the sea,
and things that moveth on the earth,
and generally beasts of all kinds,
blah blah blah blah blah blah.

And when it comes leaden round again next year,
said Sam, it will be the goddamned same.

Round it ground,
the kingdom made word,
discovering the alphabet anew anew anew,
and hammering each word into a stone
with chisels made of soap.

List, list, oh list.

And on each lap of these small masters
sat the creature they had dragged
at the chariot wheels of their secondary triumph;
their lips uncurled, their eyes awash,
their sharp bits, claws, fangs, needles, stings,
poisons, probosci, tentacles, suckers, beaks,
bludgeons, horns, swords, scythes, barbs,
flukes, nails, nips, talons, hooks and scimitars,
whetting at each breast, within which tore
the ripping tugs of fear and cudgelled boredom.

'B-l-a-h b-l-a-h b-l-a-h', said Beardo,
'B-l-a-h- b-l-a-h b-l-a-h.'
By which time dinosaurs had departed the earth.
The students sighed, O endless dullness,
O still point of turning time that will not bloody turn,
O eternal oratory! O save us!
And the creatures leaned,
shivering with intended eyes,
towards their lightly clothed humanity,
like the bodkins of a mighty sewing-machine.

Surely that is Dee, bleeding at his placket, I said.
A Snapping Shrimp quested sharply amongst his pants.
Alas, where is his knowledge now, said Sam.
I had no idea. I supposed it might be flying,
in its multiplying majesty, in other worlds.
It is flying in its multiplying majesty, said Sam,
in other worlds. Was instruction efficaceous,
and my journey too? I had hopes.

And their hope is only this, said Sam.
That their chamber turns upon a screw,
unfortunately the slowest screw known to man
or the denizens of any other universe,

theoretical or actual, and they are rising to glory
at a depressing velocity.

SONG 69 · *where they leave Bower 2 / and find a Contralto Piharau attending a
heart-shaped leaf / and are taken upwards with a mediocre song*

The bracken brush slapped my hairy shanks.
Perhaps it was a reminder.
You see I have remembered it.

Ah, we are out.
Sam lifted the velarium of his glasses.
Time for a bullseye.
He drew from his pocket two sweeties
each wrapped in a white cellophane skirt.
Yum, he said. We navigated the bouncy bough,
whilst a little dancing cloud of pepper and mint
went fragrantly before us.

Oo, Minties! said a swoony syrinx-sound,
fluteling a little nearer than we thought.
Whatever that means.
Sam swashed aside a fangle of dangled leaves.
Fuck me Jesus, he said.
For there stood a shiny Piharau,
perilously upright and pouting
upon a heart-shaped leaf.
Oh may I have one,
it sang like Pleasant Point honey.
Please unwrap for I have no arms.
It sucked with pleasant rumination.

We boarded the cordate and drifted upward,
propelled by the fluctuating notochord
while sucking and shattering its treat,
and singing the below in a fume of
volatile blooms and subtle vapours:

The ways through which my salty tail I guide,
In this delightful land of Hope,
Are so exceeding spacious and wide,
And sprinkled with such a sweet kaleidoscope
Of all that is pleasant to ear or eye,
That I nigh ravished with rare thoughts' delight,
My tedious travel do forget thereby;
And when I start to feel decay of might,
It strength to me supplies, and cheers my spright.

Which is from *sprightly*.

SONG 70 · *they land near Bower 3 / Sam's discomfort explained / they enter the Bower*

We landed exactly nice
like a powderpuff on a puff of powder.
Love, though coloured off,
seemed to be in the air.
We bid the Piharau goodbye.
He waved his scales,
twinkling with slime and mintmusk,
and oscillated outwards
into the emerald haze.

Hope, said Sam exasperated,
breathes its blasted pink breath.
And Love its purple reek.

Shall we go back, I said.
For charity.

There is enough virtue here
to float a fucking boat, he cried.
Maybe a midget's coracle merely so far,
but it is the stain of a brighter morning.
Help me over this cypress hurdle.

I took his arm and we jumped *a deux.*

Amongst certain salvation
and the cracks of hope,
dear Sam declined.
Little glows of sunlight broke upon
his splendid hair, and his intent,
undone in dark and going on there,
laboured in the broader air of gain,
eternalised by physics.

Thanks to that slimy mendicant bastard,
said Sam, throwing open the following wicket gate
at Bower 3.

Behold, for he still had his wits and night enough,
and liked a stage or two, The Bad at Love!

SONG 71 · *Bower 3 described / where the Bad at Love circle a consort of ouds / their*
ears pierced with cactus spines / singing in search of the unheard song

There, there afloat upon classical cloudlets,
one each exactly, tinged with orange and flame,
sat a million-consort of glittering ouds,
fingered by folks in flimsy fustian,
in other words veiled all in blue.

A little like musical blueberry tents, I thought.

On marmalade blancmanges.

And all about them,
from burning boff to brass-bronzed puff,
swam the Bad at Love,
all up and down the vasty tube,
and mutilated according to their kind.

For they could not hear,
(who had cast off love present;
who had put on love absent)
(which Sam said, but longer)
being pierced in each drum
with a white cactus spine,
that glittered athwart them
like the last ray of their hearts' diverted headlights.

And they cooed and they warbled,
trilled, crooned, carolled and cantillated
till their heart-strings tautened to fire
and burned at their blood.

They seek the song of the ouds, said Sam,
a little sad I thought, though he was not one for love,
for when in happenstance they harmonise,
all with all, one atom of their sourding spines
falls clink and gone into the abyss.

Which I could not think would ever surely happen
very often.

SONG 72 · *and who are they that play? / an awful moment*

And who are they that play, I asked Sam.
Are they angels?

Angels, my arse, said Sam.
They are the shrouded glimpses of a finer world
where these condemned for nearly ever
hold in every other part of time.
Did you not count them? he snarled.
They match exactly.

You see, he said after a moment,
with something like a little sigh,

we are half way now to the top.

They are a kind of hope then, I said.
Sam looked weary.
The cloudy lights of tangerine and copper
reddled about his sober suit.
His glasses, like two suns,
blazed out the beauty of his hopeless eyes.

And where they are is no place for me.
For here I am a fool,
and so must fly.

Sam! I cried. O Sam, who will guide me now?
For he was already going.
I could tell by the elevation of his shoes.

Dear, dear Sam! Don't leave me!

One begins to be very tired, he called,
as he floated upwards into the jaffary luminescence.
How one hoped, on and off, above.
With what diversity.

And poff! he was gone.

SONG 73 · *grief*

But in vain I raised without hope
my eyes to the sky to look for the Bears.
For the light I stepped in put out the stars,
assuming they were there,
which I doubted,
remembering the clouds,

Sam said.
But only in some memory of love.

I cried bitter tears.
I staggered back from the floating million-foam,
lurching like perturbed sausages on their tympanical skewers,
and shreiking at their lottery of unction.

The oudish orchestra flailed at its perfect gold beauty.

I fell at the wicket gate and broke it.
I remained on my knees and sobbed.

Had I now to leave my dearest vanities,
to be led by the hand by some gleaming ninny
to the uppermost reaches of light?
For he had been my style so, dearest Sam,
to be cleansed of for nothing,
to witness some dancing prurient goodenoughs,
singing the hymns of selfglorious virtue on high
in a language as plain as porridge?

Damned if I would.

Damned.

I fell to the moss of the branch
and blubbered in a snivelling grizzle,
alone at the end of human wishes.

SONG 74 · *the distant song of Eee, Eff, Gee and Aitch / the arrival of a gondola of fern / punted by a Karuhiruhi / but who is the new guide within?*

Tralala, came an unquiet quartet,
sadly distant at my literary ears,
and Tralala again.

How out of tune.
How could they salvage respect
from such clamouring humility?

It was surely Eee, Eff, Gee and Aitch.
Swooping unmelodiously in an orange tingement,
guessing at the wishes of some perfect, musicked thing.

I knew, for I had loved them all,
and they had sung to me in the sunset.

I had not the slightest idea really how they felt about me however.

And I had not even the discernment to hear
should an atom fall from their adamantine pins.

Anyway, I was sick of language and did not care.

I wiped my eyes on my bush-tartan sleeves.
Snot gathered in the cuffbuttonholes.

At which point a large gondola of fern hove into view
through the emerald jacket of the world-trunk.
And here is your new man,
cried down a long white-throated Kāruhiruhi,
who was punting at the liquid air with a rather laboured air,
bobbing its beak and the pole in its wing,
and a small smell of kawkawa on its breastfeathers.
Ark!

Who could it be?
I was beside myself.
Boo-hoo, I cried.

SONG 75 · *the new guide described / the novice is wary and more / the ascent to*
Bower 4

The quartet hummed,
Baa baa, black sheep.

It stepped from the gondola of fern.

Good God, what wide and hooded Simple was this,
descending in frivolous pastoral-biblical?
What dull messenger of virtuous plain and prose
to buckle and chain at my writing hands?
What shite.
How dare, in its trinketed cap and gussets,
to witness dear Sam to the judgement.
Bastard.

For it glided in foot-mist from fern-boat to bole-branch,
swirling in beanie, fatvest and boots,
and bearing, oh gutless and guilty!
in its allblack mudded mittens
a dangly-coughing lambkin!
Ugh.

Gidday, it said, which was less disappointing,
and managed my hand warmly
amongst the wee electric tail,
which could not be argued.

I countered.
Fuck off, I said,
I shall climb on alone.
I shook at its hand to dislodge its intent.
You see I missed Sam so dearly.

But it led me softly to the waiting, wafting thing,
and I followed this obsolescent eiderdown,
irresistible semishiny allweather waterproof dulldull so.
The Kāruhiruhi clapped its bended beak servicably.
Going oop, it said.
Good-oh.
I am sure Sam would have had other words for it.
And perfectly better.

We hove away into luminous green,
but, to my mind, dismal prose.

Haha, cried Eye and Jay,
we are going up to darkness.

I felt much the same, I am sure.

I knew them from school I think.
At least their knees were familiar.

They were passing by upon an ingenious omnibus
made of a large hīnau leaf, upon which
a large hīnau leaf arched from end to end,
this topped at its cap by a large hīnau leaf,
the whole thus resembling something I can't think of
going up into darkness.
This contraption, plunging pleasantly in the limey air,
a little slower than we, stirred with gentle intent
by a pair of warbling Katipōs in top hats,
crowded on its double decks its hardly saved
in shipment and in song.

Buoyed on benefacted prayers,
We rise about the woody stairs.

Well, perhaps it was interesting to know the cause at least.
I was toyingly tempted to rhyme *love* and *above*.

O happy schoolfriends, hail, well met!
Warbling in your wagonette!
May you find your harbour dear!
and, fading, they cried, We are near ...

We passed them with a complimentary wingbeat or two,
in genteel acceleration,
and landed upon the shady boughs
of Bower 4.

Bower 4, squawked the Kāruhiruhi.
Mind the shade.

You see I had ignored it nearly up to now
and kept walking.

SONG 77 · *the novice makes another attempt to discover the identity of his new guide / they enter Bower 4 by a black nailed door attended by Kay / whose fortune lay in the misfortune of another / the darkness within the Bower of Schadenfreude*

We disembarked. It with its smoking gumboots,
and I in several grumps.

With whisper and wilful thump,
wriggle cough waggle bleat,
we passed the branch's length.
While the gondola sailed like a hanky of silk
softly down the zephyrish waft,
shimmering emerald-jet for the Kāruhiruhi's back.

I looked at it sideways-sly,
my unbidden, unwanted companion.
It seemed, perhaps, to be thoughtless Youth,
so I asked for its innocent days.
Nothing. Nope. Zip.

It seemed in the hopeful business of sheep,
so I asked where its watch-box lay.
Zero. Zilch. Duck.

Suddenly, a wee black door in the trunk, knobbled with nails,
swung open like some darkling dwarf-horror,
squeaking through waves of misted swirl.
Welcome, said Kay, where all is dark.
What, I cried. You? Here?
Off-course, he smiled blackly,
mopping and mowing about our entering boots.

In happy hour did I not win
the Awesome August Anniversary Mount Hutt Slalom
when Dargaville Dan snapped his favourite legs,
and you a free-falling third?

And still the smile, like black lippaint,
gloss of silent words, ached him to distraction.

And all was dark indeedy.
And the black paint wrote his length
of hidden laughter in the hate of other men.
And it was not the darkness of nothing,
but the darkness of everything.

I cannot remember for the life of me who came second.

SONG 78 · *where the Joyful-of-misfortune mill laughably in the dark / to make
the topless ladder of their deliverance / and how the novice could see in the dark
/ which the new guide explains briefly*

How Sam would have loved it.

All this milling about, and such collisions,
ah, these hammerings at random,
mistakes of bones for stiles
and skull for rung,
and such a little nailed-up pile
of living ladder,
honky-wonky in the dark,
which fortuitously I could see,
with the blood black and the eager clamber
but three feet of its million,
and the falling over and falling down
which is really always the funniest of anything.

Oops a daisy!
Crash! Whoa!

Ah, wretched rungs!
Ah, sacrificial stiles!

Elle! Em! Enn!
Oh! Oh! Oh!
How they plummet.
And pick up the pieces.
And plummet again.

Tell me, I said, turning to the sizeable-sized stripling,
who hovered about my side like motorised lagging,
carrying the lamb in brave brave arms,
how can I see this bloody building?
For I know I am in darkness,
and yet visible is
each lost soul about its blind business.

And it put off its Colin-Clout-cap,
and said, with a head I shall tell you of soon,
'It is *their* darkness.'

SONG 79 · *the new guide shows herself / her identity / and her intent to be shiny*
with Hope

So. It was a promise.
She removed her star-knit headgear altogether.

Ah, it was She and Youth indeed!
Weatherburn moonface and great scarlet ears.
Bumpkin wavy-hair thick as spilled carpetweave.
Bucktooth and broadbum, pustular with promise.
And a dim-eyed divine dumbness,
that had not inhaled of death,
and had the innocent hope of the lamb.

Oh, Sam!

Revelations hung in the pastures, lawns and trees.
And the seat of her corduroys shiny
from Huntaway, ATV and Quad!
Such careless care of the flock.
Such thoughtless thought for the meek.

I could barely look.
For the whole seemed like long-lovely ago,
and a kind of giant promise
that weighed my heart with a golden feather,
a stamping forth of endless empty days,
and hither and thither a honeysuckle or two,
sucked like a toy trumpet in a summer haze.

Are you an Allegory? I enquired.
I'm Joy, she said. And this is Lineout.
I leaped a little sideways.
The dog growled at my ankles.
Shit a bloody brick! Whence had this new horror trotted?
Come on boy, said Joy, and with me!

With what melancholy feet of innocence
did I follow then. For this was Hope itself,
because it had not come to find intent.

Splintering bone-song faded in their darkness,
and we strode out from the nailed door to the general shine.

I'm the light, said Joy. Why would you shade me?
Let's go. And we all did.

SONG 80 · *Joy explains plainly why it is now that she has come / the novice wrestles with the light / and takes a pair of offered sunnies*

And why must you come now, I asked peevishly,
while things got on so nicely?

Hope is plain, said my heart for her answer there,
but not simple. How else could your bright friend
have calculated his exact unfitness?

This was cruel, I thought,
though perfectly right, and my own.

He was not taken lightly, then? I asked,
as we emerged upon a brilliant bough,
where I shaded my eyes in expectation
of a Sam-wise burst of braininess.

I have, said she,
cuddling the wet little patient to her breast,
just that exactly Hope that he had not.
It was a good swap.
Lineout snapped at my socks
and went grrrrrrr.

I squinted metaphysically.
Ah, too much of light.

Jew want these? said Youth.
What was she at,
in that undamnable frame of a vast farm?
From what tubby nook they came,
plastic, wraparound and not my choice,
I took these shades and put them on.

Was it the practicality of this newness,
or maybe merely kindness
from a sympathy of souls?
I did my very best to smile. A little ghastly.
Behind the blinding of my obvious eyes.

Ta.

Yor welcome.

It is no sin to follow simplicity.
It is not that much fun.
It is a moot matter whether Hope
cometh from a necessary blindness,
or the threshing-floor of intelligence.

I followed however, exasperatedly eager behind
the liquid ebony of my specs.

A large luteolin leaf
slung beneath the leeward legs
of two kirtled kōkakos
by a pleached toetoe and a thorn nail or two,
swung like a swingboat by our knees
in a tranced emerald breath.

We were aboard, and rose rapt
with organ-bells and tolling catches,
which was their song of joy,
up, up to a great branch shone with soap
and all aglitter too.

And who are these? I asked my new man,
suddenly alit, who slither squealing down the bough
towards their bright and bitter bower.
Grrrrrrr, said Lineout, biting at my bootlaces.
These Pees, I enquired, and Queues?
These Ares, these Esses, that I knew?

They are the Vain, she said, who have
their sunny-far salvation in their very sin.
How so, said I,

watching while they passed, who had not fallen,
through a silver door suddenly and unsubstantial.
I mean *through* a door. That was not open.

Way-hay! cried dear Joy, there goes another one!
It clawed and slapped upon the soap
and fell down, down through the jellied aura of the bole.

Ah, I said enjoyingly. That will be the ladder then.

SONG 82 · *the Bower of the Vain described / how their sin is their saviour / and
how they must crawl, heavy with masks, in a diamante maze*

We entered like smoke. Within,
the sob and sigh beneath turned my eyes
down.

Where, in a maze that glittered shallow as glass,
the semi-damned butted and crawled
hither and thither and there and back,
cracking mistaken in some multitudinous motherboard
of walls and winkled ways
to find their freedom.

They have persisted in their sin, said Joy, trying,
preferring overpraise to their own eyes: but
knowing this has saved them, for they were ashamed
before themselves beneath their — masks.

Look close.

I did. And each amongst the coruscating sparkled walls
slouched and grovelled with heavy head: and each
face fixed fast in some fulgurating otherface nodding
in a ton of glitz.

How will they escape, I asked,

hanging to my own goddamning facewear,
amazed at the simplicity of my concern.

One glittered thing will find a way
in every thousand years. And in the rhyming light
of The Good Place
their massy mask will melt.

The tiny clishing of their blinding growths
against the towered walls of ice.

Bark, said Lineout, bristling happily.

SONG 83 · *they sit upon the soapy bough for lunch / the novice speaks to Tee,*
who clambers to his punishment / and falls / the kōkakos ring their bells in
understanding

We can share this eggy pie, said the youth.
Which came from I shudder to think,
and the naked pastry hot on her large lactic lap.
We swung our legs and gobbled ow ow ow
a steam of steak and Hohepa Herb Quark,
and let the lamb lick and the doggie dine.
Why do we not fall? I asked gasping gulp.
Because the falling is not meant for us,
or the soap for our still heart-beating souls.

Which seemed sensible, and not badly put.
Though the glory of cleverness dies in longing,
it was not here that it was any more.
At which the big branch bounced and bibbled,
and a clutch of tottering fame
clambered by. Some slipped and toppled away
with a dying fall. Others teetered tardigrade
along the pinguid pole.

Surely that is Tee! I gasped, who

left Tapawera for a mess of golden graces!

Talk to him while he flutters, said Joy,
which was almost as fine as dear Sam, but more brown.

Would you like this bit of pie that is left?
I said to Tee. Is hunger a part of the death of vanity?
He panted and gazed sadly up. Already
the bunions of glass were began,
knobbling pimpled about his cheeks.

Creeping to my sightless land
I yearn – he lost his foot, his hand –
For what, dear soul? He fell.
Regret is very hell.

A hot steak gobbet tumbled with him asteam.

The kōkakos rang their gorgeous bells,
who will be back with him upon the slippery bough
in a hundred years.

SONG 84 · *the swifter passage toward Bower 6 / an incredible light from Joy and Above / the tiny dancing glitter glimpsed atop all*

We sucked our fingers
and our paws.
Then we held hands and negotiated the last saponifications
to the leafy landing pad.

Joy the shepherd leaned meatily on a stipule.
This'll be awesome, she smiled.

Awesome indeedy.

An amber sycamore helicopter
piloted by two velvet-blue whai repos

descended crackling from an indigo cloud.
Electric emanations zapped
from their flesh-tails aflick
and drove the rotorblades
in a frenzy of manipulatable power.

They landed bouncingly beside.
Bower Ssssssix, they hissed as one
and smiling from their forward flukes.

We hurtled up and up along the very border
of the mighty tree's tops' emerald aura.
Blades of electricity chopped and zagged about us
like whips of regal razorwire.

We zoomed to starboard. Light streamed
from Joy's gob agape.
Shall my shield melt now haha, I said.
You will die too, and come to it somewhere,
she said, in spite of truth and beauty.
Grrrrr, said Lineout, licking his choplets.

Golden rays surged out between her teeth,
and her Alfred E. Neuman ears.

The helicopter ballooned towards its port.
And in that moment I glimpsed, atop the great tree,
the tiny dancing glitter of unabandoned hope.

SONG 85 · *the novice and his guide pass into Bower 6 / the Theorists / which is
described / the novice descries You and prepares to go down to her*

The road was broad and barky:
the gate, however, a small pastry-cutter.

Through this sweetly scalloped circle
we watched the flaying calves of Theoretical Men

drawn in with exquisite pain.
We passed
with only a slight frilling about our edges.

Oh brrrr, said my guide agrin,
her corrugations unundulating
by some lantern-air within,
that made her all shine
like an ear backlit with candles.

Look, she said. Here are the men
who tidied the world with their thoughts;
upon whose theories much died
that did not fit.

Above, before, below, a great cheese-grater
like a steel wall between the earth and space;
and in its holes the zillion struggled blood and straitened flesh
that strained against their pain to reach the happy side.

They cannot bear the pain that movement makes,
said Joy of it all. Tearing to the outer sky.

What has saved them? Ah! Dishonesty.
Why was I hardly pleased at all?

May I go down please and speak to You: she is there, there,
and so far only scalped. Nude-hung by her crown of steel.

The lamb coughed in a wee convulsion.
The shepherd rubbed its ears.
I would have patted bloody Lineout had he not
retracted to a sitting siege.
Grrrrrr.

Here is your prompt deadly sherpa, said Joy,
beaming still sky-candlelike from within.

I mounted the globular abdomen of a katipō.
Its little red stripe fired and we were off!
Scuttling upon a tiny swingbridge
that was to tell the truth one wambling wire.

Oh, vertiginous crossing!
Oh, looming ever-Everest of steel!
Oh, straps of falling flesh and blood!
Hiho Silver!

Scurrying suddenly down,
rearing at her hole like a poisonous Dressager.
O You! I called. The cutty fenestella
bit her head. I saw that she must lose her ears.
First. At least.
It is your old friend from Mt Robert.
How we skied like twins two by two
down the powder slopes. Our poles
so sweetly swung in unison all day
until the sunset painted red the snow we loved.

Mmmm mmmm mmmm, and blood fell forth.

I care not what you did,
what knife you took to the world
for thinking what you thought: have hope,
ah, friend of my childhood, have hope
in this, your most black black hour,
for there will be an end to this, not soon,
not nearly in a while, but far later,
when you will come, all half-undone and red
to happiness deserved, when in that doubtful night

you put the lamps all out
and knew, thank goodness, your confusion.

Mmmmmmm MMMMMMM, and that was tears.

How terrible that this exhortation
tore half a hundredth inch against dear You's shaved skull,
though in the right direction.

SONG 87 · *the katipō carries the novice and his guide out of Bower 6, western-*
style / they wait in the gleaming air for their last carriage / and hear the music
of the tiny dancing glitter / till the ship arrives

Yee-ha! cried Joy's voice from far away.
The katipō rattled back across its wire.
I wiped away the water in my eyes
caused by such speed through cold and metal air.

Ride 'em cowboy! Up she hoofed behind,
lamb and Lineout and all.
The katipō clattered squealing
through the cutting-gate and out upon the wood.

We sat together all four
upon a twiglet and enjoyed the verdant aura
and the lukewarm lolling of the –

Listen! I cried. A gentle tingle-tangle.
Like a chandelier of diamonds in a zephyr.
Like music that was twinkle.
Like glittery melodious.

It is the twingle of the dear Pohutukawa
and its little burst of scarlet sun, said Joy with a smile.
We are near.

Grrrrrrr, said Lineout. I moved not.

This was aramaic to me.
Was I to journey amongst the transports of joy
in the keeping of a vegetable?

O Joy! Am I to journey amongst the transports of joy
in the keeping of a vegetable? I enquired.
The strapping shepherd tapped the side of her pimpled nose
thrice.

Do not trust in your own understanding bow wow.

We were saved from the parliaments of faith
by the arrival of our last great white billowing floaty ship,
which hove upon us in a harmony of kōtares.

SONG 88 · *which is given entirely to a description of the last great white galleon,
which is worth it / oh, and a tiny revelation*

Lineout licked my upper socks without kindness.

The ship we sat in, clapp't in milk-white yew,
flew on bulgéd sails of cloven cream,
in company of sapphire kingfishers
who silent darted 'mongst the bannered masts
of bleachy pine. About the gunnels peered
a thousand crowded faces of the nearly
blessed, each in satin crown and cotton
cloak. Upon the castle's alabaster
bricks the captains stood, three Pāpahus,
their hundred smiling teeth and wetblack coats
all shining in the crystal thoughts of foam,
whilst all about our ears vanilla swirled,
stirred by long albescent oars, whose masters,
merry Millipedes in rhythmic voice
and glass tiaras, steered us through the green
and jellied atmosphere, while we, our eyes

hand-shaded at the mizzen-mast, peered forth
in hope of hope for all who live their term
between the myriad worlds of time that damn
or save us for eternity, to this
last Bower, through a rain of softened glass.
Oh Joy, sweet lamb and shepherd, this will be
my own damnation; and your plainer kindness
shows me true and saves me in its sight.

Oh specks of life, enjoy your summer all:
and run to this, your long night's festival.

SONG 89 · *the novice questions Vee, Dubblew and Exe concerning Bower 7 / the*
Romantics / they disembark

Ahoy, where sail ye, Vee, Dubbleyew and Exe?
Why caught, and why not damned?
I had seen then singing on the sternrail,
catching the light of hope on their distant skulls,
and uncertain of their awe,
from Collingwood, Pakawau and Rockville?

I turned my jet lenses at their plushed and quiet crowns.

We sail to soonest night,
and to the Tree of Love,
whose darkest song is bright,
who blooms in bliss above.

The great white ship ground upon the high-smaller branches
of the great green tree, and came upon its harbour.
Gangplanks slapped upon the potscour bark,
and off they came, tripping to their shrouded ...

They are the Sad Romantics, said sympathetic Youth,
though Joy-unJudged, who peopled Nature
with their mental Nymphs, and vested goodness

in the meanest flower, and schooling in the grass.

What impness is there in this starry green? I asked,
luminously verdant as I was,
and all about.

Let's have a dekko, said she, for whom
a theory was a hundred sights
with no conclusion.
And had I learned that right?

We followed in a train of soiling cotton gowns,
into a briar hedge.

SONG 90 · *they enter Bower 7 through the needle-brake / the Bower and the greeting of the Sad Romantics described*

The soft condemned charged as one
upon the barrier of bristling briar,
rending their robes, chopping their crowns,
and we with them untattered,
as they were not thorns for us.

This much I had learned,
and had no need to ask.
What is a miracle of deliverance
may be the changing moment
of another's swift deserts:
and the intent merely physics
and the stings of conscience.

And being dead of course.

Lookie look, said Joy.
All the world a wooden stair
that wound about the universe of stars
within the mighty trunk. Atop,

the faintest fizz of flickering fulguration.

Ahhh, and Oooo, said the sad ones.

Who were greeted by a battery of baa-lambs
that butted them from their bosky balcony
into the daffodilly deeps.

Awesome, said Joy, as we watched
Exe particularly tumble to the first
countable stair, down down down into the darkness,
and too deep for tears.

Will the wee lamb die, I asked, amongst their health.
I shall carry him, said Joy, wherever he goes.

I who had scoffed, could not moralise this.

Grrrrr, said Lineout amongst the flowers.

SONG 91 · *they watch the emergence of Vee, Dubblew and Exe through a useful infra-red telescope / the activity upon the great staircase*

Try this, said a maculate merino, and weep.

Do you have twenty cents? said Joy.
I mosied in my corduroys.
Yes, I said.

The eye of the telescope slapped up
like the eye of a waking dragon.

I took my turn.
There, in ghosted black and white
began the trial of my aching friends.

Vee came first, his eyes like silver coins,

sightless from the brilliant burst of
my lovely tapetum lucidum.
His underwater greyness – whoa!
And what was that upon his olden-movie back?
A stupendous sack of skylarks screaming
at his age-empausing first sweet step.
He did not make it in the hour I watched.
And only many million still to make.
And by each hour the burden rots and suppurates,
dragging with its putrid counterforth
against the mounting of the man.

And Dubblew dragging by its chains
a field of shortly golden wheat,
and Exe the logging wealth of Mangarakau
stacked upon his head.

I lowered my vision of this night,
and saw the higher reaches of the stair:

where carcasses of bees and nightingales,
and mould of leaf and rot of flower
hung like lumpish, cumbrous snot
upon their million messengers,
and caught, here on a broken beak, and there
in a slime of stooks, the tiniest of glances
of the tiniest of lights.

SONG 92 · *hope and light / Joy the shepherd prepares to pass away / the novice*
thinks

And does this little sight of light
fleet the feet of those nearly there? I asked,
tilting down the coolblack tube
to view the top-escaping few,
or is it as some awful taunt,
depressing into slower motions
the footsteps of these freighted friends?

Both, said Joy, bright, unfazed
and brushed upon the knobbles of her warmer
by the pale and far gleamed paint
of that little thing that we had seen,
and soon might meet.

We are alive, said Joy, despite the lamb,
and I have soon to go away and live,
being young and full of brilliant plans,
and you, by how I do not know,
to take your privilege and preview here
beyond the dancing of the little light
that separates the better from the good.

Which was not philosophy, and might have been
the contents of my simple thoughts transferred.

It was here I wondered first if I bestrid the world,
and this could be my poem.

Language, vision, light and all.

We shook the clees of several sheep,
and left the vasty, creaking stair
to seek the transcendental air.

SONG 93 · *they climb the silver ladder to the issue of Bower 7 / where Why emerges / his rapturous reception described*

Climb oh climb the silver ladder,
To the Better from the Badder;
Tingle tangle bing and bong,
It will not take you very long.

Truly, I said to Youth, a singing ladder.

Yep, said Joy. Things sing

to show the way to man when he is lost.
But not where we live. There,
man sings to himself in trees.

However, the silver ladder sang true,
for I had no sooner put my boot upon the bottom rung
than I was elevated to the great tree's shining crown.

We swayed in the circle of a mile, yet seemed upright.
We flibbled in the whitest of light, yet seemed unexposed.
We heard the sound of a triangle bingbing, yet knew all was quiet.

At which moment exactly, Why emerged with a whoop-whoop
from the tiny top of the trunk, slender as a flute,
shout shout and shattering with paleblue glass.

He is come from the Vain, I thought to myself,
after a million years,
like a corpse from a glacier.

As he stood atremble, clinking and going off
in tiny explosions of imprisoning crystal,
a hundred, for I counted them, Pūtangitangi descended
flapping through waves of yellow-shine,
bearing in their heavenly bills a Moses bassinet
and trailing shrouds of flory as they came.

Oh, Why! I called, but amidst his poppings and his tears
he heard me not, transported by transport.

And Lineout's loppy ears went flop. Down.

They scooped him in the bassinet
and laved him deep in winceyette,
and took off with their banners bright
all twirling 'mongst the honey-light.
And we, both seeming-winged, attended,
grinning while we all ascended
far beyond the final Bower,
Pūtangitangis for an hour.
Our feathered breasts like knightly armour
gleamed with catalytic karma,
trumpeting our honking thrill,
apoetheo-majestical.

Whilst from the wicker
shards of glass
went ping! and pung!:
his riving mask.

What you have seen on ceilings painted,
royal, legal, naval, sainted,
comes not near the streaking fires
bursting round in amber gyres,
nor the waves of musicked air
everywhere, oh! everywhere!

And thus we came, with all the briefness
of briefs, briefcases and breviaries,
into the presence of the little fizzing light,
the wee midge made diamond,
which in fact was
a light-feathered kiwi
feathered with light.

Ah, so much light.
Hail, glorious light!

Welcome, it whistled, and then, Hack hack.

Why bowed low, not in obeisance
but in natural gratitude.

I'm very pleased to be here, yelled Why
in a fountain of tears,
and fell down in a flat bloody faint.

SONG 95 · *the novice bids farewell to Joy, Lineout and the Lamb / the end of the*
sunglasses / an invitation to The Good Place

Good, said Joy herself, satisfied with that,
and now I'm off.

She approached me with some purpose.
Just when I was growing to love you, I said.
I'll have those, she replied,
and reached my shades away,
whose black-ink-rivered lenses dropped,
like liver from a plate,
their black-oil shapes upon the grass.

If you're ever passing Ranzau Road,
call in for a beer.

And when I looked up,
the company of Hope and Youth
were vanished in the last-lit heel
of some unqualified intent.

I waited for tears that did not come.

It is time, said the Golden Kiwi,
nodding about in its brightness,
its feathers going zizz and whoosh in lambent plumes.
We will go to The Good Place now,

if you take me in both hands gently,
as if I were an egg.

Are you? I said.
Or the chicken?

The Golden Kiwi tapped the side of his probey beak thrice.
Both, hack hack, he replied.

I came to him with a nest of two hands.

SONG 96 · *the glorious journey upon the Golden Kiwi described*

I bent softly to this loveliest of creatures,
and he hopped upon my trembling palms.
His eye that I could see black-beady bright.
His rudimentary wings afluffle in his sides of orpiment.

How shall we go, I asked in a vanilla breath
that I did not usually have, when you cannot fly?

I may not be able to fly, he smiled,
but by God I can run.

At this, the Golden Kiwi began the one-two one-two
of his little cinnamon legs, which increased in frequency,
creating, after a minute or two, a kind of latent whirr,
his six copper claws skimming, like magic razors,
my stratum corneum, with barely a whispered wind,
and turning, after some minutes more,
his raw-umber arse towards my burning wrists.

Follow me, he whistled.
Fare close in my slipstream, he honked
above the noise of his revving leggies.
We shall sprint at the speed of light!

I had enough physics to know that certain death
would follow my Lorenz-FitzGerald Contraction
and the approach of infinite mass.
I was inclined to fat besides.

With a farted flame and an apparent engagement of gear,
the Golden Kiwi shot sideways into the lemon sky,
and I, joining the expanding universe, was sucked away behind.
Way-hay! I cried amidst such protected acceleration
that my head launched flames like the sun.

We rose too fast to know. Butterflies filled my self.
And amidst the ambering air, his little legs
blurred in a goldensyrupy splendour before me.

SONG 97 · *the glorious journey continues / the Golden Kiwi explains the
endurantic and perdurantic nature of time and space*

As we approached the speed of light,
various friendly photons became distinguishable,
and their tiny bright smiling faces betrayed no labour
in the massless flight of their tiny packets.

They do not speak, please note, but communicate
by the affectation of two expressions: 1 and 2.

Brrm Brrrrmmm, said the kiwi. Here we go!
At which point everything went black
in a visible way, and we silently sped on the spot
as the world which we could not see passed us
in both directions invisibly.

It was bloody great.

Now, said the glorious luminous wee beast,
his little flight-denying feathers ruffled in all directions,
and not at all disturbed by an undisturbing light,

to the matters of Time and Space.

We cruised beyond speed, beyond everything except a colour
that was all the more joyous for not being there.

Have we three dimensions or four?
Do we have merely spatial parts, or temporal too?
And do we exist always wholly, or on and off?

I was buggered if I knew, or, at such wonder, cared.
He answered himself swiftly, believing the timeless space
that I did not take not to answer,
was the messenger of confusion.

Hahaha, he whistled through his beak-trils.
Both.

For to come to The Good Place, we must — ooops!
We hurtled at, approached, landed upon, and surveyed,
all the same, er, moment, though it was not one,
what mathematicians call a Polar Rose,
which is an idea, ah, and not a bad one.

SONG 98 · *the Polar Rose described / the novice meets Zed / who shows him
the passage of his world / where the moments of sin are extinguished upon each
advance in The Better Place / a physical explanation by the Golden Kiwi / who
then vamooses*

There really is no time to sing
all the parts of this song.

Being a beautiful thought, this million-tiered phantasy
lay upon bright nothings in a gossamer-crystally way,
upon the outermost petal-round of which,
a bleached shade of buttercup,
vibrated unmoving in the absent air,
we stood, undulating in motionless bliss.

Where also was Zed, having recently also landed
with the Golden Kiwi in a separate time-space continuum.
He was draped in a eggyolk poncho
and overcome with selfish celebration.

Twenty thousand billion years I have climbed,
driven, dragged, spliced and screwed myself
towards this dreamed-of end. And ten years more it took
to be completely cleansed at the silver flute's mouth.
And now I am here.
He threw out a fine, suntanned arm.
Behold! he cried, the passage of my world!

Which was a mighty tunnel wherein Zed's hours and moments
zoomed to their present like an underground train.
And why, here and there, I asked, looking from my waving sweetness,
is there a carriage missing?

They, said Zed, are the seconds of bad
negated by love
in the hope of my climb.

Leaving, said the Golden Kiwi, wreathed in sunflower bannerets,
only goodness. For we are amongst the Inertial Frame,
where perception alone gives sense, and thus may be moral.

Here and goodbye, he squeaked, may we Endure,
amidst the happy losses of Perdurantism.

Well, that's clear then. And my lightning friend
wound at his leggies once more, and walloped away.

And why has Why been withheld a whyle? I asked.
For I saw him victorious at the top of that place.

Zed frisked at the edges of his poncho,
which boiled like scrambled eggs.
He really was a happy porpoise.

He must grow again his broken body,
so that it may Endure without corruption.
You will see him if you stay here several years to wait.

We walked to the very edge of the lavender petal,
which I am sure was buttercup before.
We stood upon the glass lip of its petal-waft,
and gazed into Momentum from its Centre.

It looked like black and white. I mean at once.
And what was in between. Which was most. If not all.

I leave you here, said Zed, and go to dance
across a large expanse of pennywort
with a summer-house in the middle,
and a barbeque at the end. Thank goodness.

And he swirled away like a Swirling Dervish,
indubitably in touch, his bare feet staining delicate green
from the mighty lawn I could not see.
And a slight mist.

Where I waited in suspense. Though not long.

For in its plaintive distant twang and thud I saw
the dear Pohutukawa in its little burst
of scarlet sun
draw near.

III

THE GOOD PLACE

III

THE GOOD PLACE

SONG 100 · *the arrival of the dear Pohutukawa Tree / that anticipated vegetable guide*

Thump thump
twingle twangle
bump bump
spingle spangle
came the dear Pōhutukawa
leaf-pounamu, flower-pāua,
striding 'cross the pearly ski-glass,
hurling golden pollen this way that way
and grumbling in his search for pleasant rhymes and rhythms to
    speak with.

He hove into sight. Such thrilling flowers,
and not of language. How Sam would have hated him
for his merriness.

I hope from Hope that Joy one day will come,
to talk in bouncing rhyme with this delight.

Ah, how cruel life is in the waiting:
and the doing unnoticed,
and the dying hard.

Like a brush with a smiling photon in the dark.

Gidday, I said, in a cloud of cadmium microgametophytes.

Gidday, he replied.
This was not long enough for a blasted rhyme.

But not this:
Welcome Tourist. This way please.
Hut Eleven! For your skis!

The voice was pleasantly creak-wise,
with no boom portentous, no thunder sagacious.

And I followed his bristling scarlet hair
and hurled mad pollen-stars
around the outest petal-glassy thoroughfare.

SONG 101 · *the novice is fitted with his skis in a cuckoo clock / a reflection on life / first foray on the slopes / the gigantic wonderful view described*

With the spry step of springboard-sprung schottischers,
we marched amongst mānuka and mountain-daisies,
our roots and boots sure upon the sparse-grassed glass.
The skyblue petal waving languid with us on it,
going creek creek creeeek.

Hut Eleven was a cuckoo-clock. At its honeypine doors,
all carved with birdies and forest foliage,
hung a large chocolate clock with no hands,
as pretty as a picture. The doormat was
a slice of gingerbread spread with icing.

Two silver chains hung down into the cosmos,
clicking with a tiny intergalactic schmaltz.
I took my skis from the wall, where they hung crosswise.
Great wooden things they were, with clunk-clip bindings.
And raffia placemats on the sticks.

I looked about. The dear tree rustled happily outside.
Ah, the alpine-cuckoo hut! Ah, the joy of cod!
Ah, adventure in comfort and the other way about!
Like putting on my Tuareg slippers for a journey down the hall.

Which everybody wants.

I slapped outside. The Pōhutukawa tree
had extended its extensive root system
into a little pleached sledge, and was ready too.
We pottered for a while in the rosy glow.
Our gentle telemarks and snowploughs
sent soft showers of apple snow shaved from the glass.

Ready? said the Pōhutukawa tree. Steady?

I took a sweet deep breath before we pushed off.
Gently sloped away a million miles of shine beyond
lay the Good Place, in undulating crystal pleasances.

The first fabulous wet-creaks of pressed snow.
The gleaming invitation warbled in the far-away.

Watch my flowers, said the tree, in a schuss.
Go.

SONG 102 · *the Pōhutukawa's flowers in action / a friendly question / at the vitreous hillock / Pleasances of the Good Place explained / at the lip of No. 1*

Flowers indeedy.

As we gathered speed, hissing ecstatically along the powder-crust,
the dear Tree put on a show of prodigal pollination.

From his forty thousand flowers
flung a flare of pollen showers,
constellated inflorescence
swirled in bloomy erubescence.
Nectarous hermaphrodite,

what a bloody thrilling sight!

I crackled along with Stem Christies
in a blizzard of gold and alabaster stars.

Do you cross- or self-pollinate? I asked,
with, it turned out, a clairvoyant politeness.
It seemed a friendly way to find a friend.

He tapped his bark thrice.
Both, he said, in a long curved line,
the sledge the labour of his soulful show.

And then in quiet we enjoyed our swoosh
until we reached a vitreous glittering hillock,
which was lip to my first good Pleasance.

We swished to a parallel stop.
The dear Tree pointed a branch beyond.

The Pleasances of yon Polar Rose
are laid in luminescent rows,
retroflexed in five dimensions,
fitted with pinnate extensions,
happy homes in thought and deed
of happy men.

So down we skied.

SONG 103 · *wheeee over the hillock / Pleasance 1 described / where there is much timeless activity / they are the Biologists*

Go for your life! said the Tree,
accelerating towards the mauve frozen wave
of the glass hillock and creaking joyously.

I followed, punting my skipoles in irresponsible fury,
and hurtling at his rustling side down down and

whoooo-eeeeeeeeee!
We zoomed upon the monticle and took orf.
I looked down at a world
of half-sucked opalescent barelysugar.

The air was cool as we sped through it,
and there was time to greet each other
at the utmost of our flight,
and a little like sherbert dip.
The yellow one.

We parked parallelely. Diamond drizzle
puffed from our skis to our red cheeks.

Below us, in a limegreen sunlight,
folks bounced slowly up and down,
at run, at play, at brown study,
eternally enweaved. Who are they?

Who are they? I asked my exhilaration,
whose brushy flowers were a little wind-bent back.

Biologists, said the Tree, correcting his hair.
Who seek the truth.
I watched them greenly yoyo. Struth.

SONG 104 · *the geography of Pleasance 1 / what forever-replenished and ever
undiscovered flora and fauna the Biologists pursue with joy / a question concerning
the objectivity of scientists*

It were mostly lawns and mānuka,
green as green can be,
with a trimming of lofty tōtara,
spranglings of rock and river,
and all the niches, habitats and homelets
of plants and creatures known and unknown.

I recognised the crusty Karaka,
the proboscal giraffe weevil,
the Matuku-moana in droopy-winged flight,
the chestnut kekeno swelling on its shore.

But what in heaven's name was that?
And that buzzy swimming thing all silver-blue?
And that? And that, by God?

Behold, the undiscovered creatures
floating o'er the surf-salt beaches,
noddy-seeded flowers and grasses
whisp'ring in the mountain passes,
where these Curious boundless find
the sweet companions of mankind.

Ah, and they discovering forever,
and chasing for their documents,
all in joy and an all-suiting weather.

But, I asked the silently jangling redness,
are not the informations even of the scientist
informed by his great jealousies and loves,
his angers, pride and ecstasy?
Or is a fact, my friend, – I ventured – fact.

The dear Pōhutukawa Tree shifted
sideways to the slippery slope
and prepared to complete a circular traverse
at speed. Hahaha, he said. Both.

There is no doubt that I was certainly learning
something.

Imagine a Wall of Death made of ice,
or some glasscrystal bowl,
whose colour-phasing sides,
and this the outermost and longest thus,
bumped at the vast shined edges of its petals,
one round of which, a million miles,
was made in half an hour, and what we saw.

I believe we went clockwise, though it is not a fact,
for I think that my right leg, being at the downhill ski,
was a little more tired after.
Or it may have been the other way round.
It was bloody fast anyway.

And as we sped together, ski and sledge,
like souls upon their carcases of wood,
about the fruit-ice of this happy Pleasance,
we saw the blissed Biologists leaping slow-mo
at unheard-of butterflies in the lemon-watered sun
of early morning, or writing in their little books
whilst soaring down to the dewy lawns of home,
or following the scamper of some white-fuzzed hare
in loops of peardrop light in awed observance.

We chattered around the vasty circle,
gasping at our velocity and our juddered legs,
while turning here and there to gaze
in all this unaccustomed mango-melting time of day.

And I remember her, who in a grey embroidered jacket
sailed off the diamond lawn to clutch in nested hands
a tuatara ten feet long, with ears, and a third eye
awide and moist with fiery scents of autumn.

And Adam, bounding after camels in a waste
of wasted beauty, rose-rocked canyons
and popping atom-sand, beneath a fierce cream sun.

And Beatrice at her beetles, sailing with a little net
upon the lambent air at midday, heart aflutter
at the unseen carapace, and the unknown ant.

And Charlie, far it seemed from Upper Hutt,
sinking slowly to a study with no roof,
holding in his trembling hands the designing wheat
that made itself indispensable to man,
and thrived so, spilling blobs of flour
amongst the mighty arms of tōtara and kauri.

This was no torment, from what
to be distracted for a little while
by some visitor's unslightly chat, by some
suspected wish to share in bliss before its time,
or finger at its pathos should it never be.

And so I skied on, ball-spun in a roulette wheel,
beneath the champagne and carnation sky,
with the tree whizzing at my side, and kept my peace,
and theirs, and almost wished to die upon my race.

And I saw a great whakahā, but fifty feet and white,
gaping through the ether for flying fish.

Phew & blimey.

But honey-warm in my jersey and gabardines.

We stood on our edges and surveyed inwards.
The Pōhutukawa Tree rustled with silent hairstyling.
Our skis made little slithering chatters on the rosy glass.
And caught our breath.
Which took a little while to catch us up.
A small blackcurrant jelly,
blurbling silently at our fancies
and pricked with silvery pins and needles.

As fresh sweet water swishes our way down a plughole,
our track, in an orient pearl spiral, swung itself
quicksilvered down through wavy pleasances of hills and vales,
towards the omphalos, like a diaphanous bolus
swung by it, tied to a banner of gossamer-ice.

And the colours all, but all soft-hued,
licking-lit, it looked, from underneath,
playing like the beautiful beast of heaven
turning in his house of glass for very joy.

These are the colours of goodness, said the dear Tree
without a word. He raised several various branches,
boughs and twigs, stribbling them about softly,
his wooden dance to the music of lights.

What should I do at such a pass?
Spray a cannonade of lime jubes
out of my gob at the sun?
Fizz forth a fountain of Lezzo
by the light of a thousand candles?
Rattle up the raspberry snowstorm of Ulan Baatar

that I keep in the airing cupboard?
And oh the amber elephant!

So I waved my mittens in the coriander air
and murmured, Hail, happy livery!

The beast bent up its bright-blotch back.

SONG 108 · *some interPleasancey travellers / the novice needs not speak to*
Dawn / a little thought concerning language / how the happy can move from
Pleasance to Pleasance

What is that clickclickclick,
like knitting with ivory needles
a mountain-mantle of cellophane?

Herringboning up, which is down,
the vasty petal of our breather,
came tittering three woolly travellers,
singing thus:

Along the plenilunal mists,
We seek the bless'd Biologists:
to shake their mittens 'neath the autumn sun,
We make the Golden Journey to Pleasance 1.

And on they came, snip snap snip snap,
beanies, goggles, scarves ablow, parkas, skipants,
boots, bindings, slip slap slip slap slap slap stop.

Shirley that is Dawn from the Fishing Club, I cried,
and thirty years between Mata'utu and Surabaya
in a Laughing Loon Custom Canoe!
How was creation there?

Through her gaspy grin the liquorish waft of breath
needed not words, for in it lay

knowledge of wood and weevil.

And the beautiful burden of language,
so dear to dear Sam, and blithely carried otherwise,
so golden-stiff when the struggle is done,
what is it but man's call upon the silence of his world
that is its own reply and satisfaction,
there being none from it,
and a turning to each other.

And can the happy call upon one another
in this place, or are they merely moving
in their minds amongst some general joy?
I asked the Pōhutukawa Tree.
You can imagine now his answer,
which word began with B.

SONG 109 · *over the icehill to Pleasance 2 / the vision of Those who Loved a Place from afar / a little ramble concerning language once more*

At this, he flung his sledge into the sudden slope
and with a Whoop plunged at the Holmenkollen
ahead, pollen flying in frozen swarm-clouds,
streaming in my way vanilla-spiked,
like madness and laughter,

                                        and I followed after.

There is a speed at which a man gives up caring,
for he knows that it is no control of his
that keeps him at the course uncrashed;
and this we passed, the tree being no man,
in the first mere yard of our career.
In the environment of a mathematical idea,
I was persuaded that my perception
was physically, that is, in the sense of physics,
our present and ever-accelerating speed.

Which may, extrapolated, be maybe life's Essence.

Wham! Off we took.

Look! cried the Tree, its branches all backwards,
like the woody banners of a woody charging army.
The idea was that he was pointing down,
where I looked as we sailed, rather faster,
though it seemed still.

What on earth is that? For below

I saw a happiness of discs
like fluctuating asterisks,
swirling over rosy hills
like gyroscopic daffodils,

like jellyfish twining in a whirlpool,
like whirling mushrooms with skirts lit
with discolights that —
oh bugger this.
For language outdoes the things of the earth
and even, I have learned, of better places.

It is all the more hard thus to relinquish
the pride of it.

SONG 110 · *Those Who Loved a Place described / their portable transports of
joy / their colour-burbling worlds*

They are – ah! ah! ah!' (this from the light-speeded air,
being cold-rose between his twiglets) Those Who –
oo! oo! oo!' (and this from the sheer exhilaration
of a Wooden Heart several miles above its own evolution)
Loved a – ha! ha! ha! (and this in turn from
a coinstantaneous appreciation of flying by one
who was made not to, and the sure belief of invulnerability,

which we in Nelson call angels)
play-hey! hey! hey! hace!

Who have travelled or stayed at home
bound to the world, and known it,
glorying in an earth that does not love back,
and human souls who may, or may not,
whatever.

There, is that plain enough for you?

And there they were, as we came in to land
through the scent of Monoï Tiaré
rubbed on a breaching whale,
glorious spinning tops of fluctuating

— oh 'struth,

can language fail before a sight no less than real?
And must I say words fail me, and bear
the scoldings of dear Sam, who thought them more
than any lack of hope the world could afford?

Yuss. Come on.
Buckle up. Buckle down.
Imagine a million million million million million
Whoiling Doivishes, each in a skirt as big as the Pacific,
turning in bliss in a sky of rose, one arm up, one down,
slowly yet strangely quickly spun,
their great red felt hats the flibbling coalfires
of their hearts and souls,
and on their jubbahs' ocean waves gleaming –

I shall need another Song, though it is going quite well.

and on their jubbahs' ocean waves gleaming, turning,
ahem, as when the solar wind, sent from heaven's sun,
splashes 'gainst Earth's upper gasses spun
with bright electrons, protons (I have spoke
to one of them, remember?) and a smoke
of art-electric discharge energising
O and N, and thus envitalising
colours oh! what colours! madly star-kiss't,
rare aurora rutilant australist!

Except that it was made out of places,
that is, there is Etera with a dress of Paterau,
worbling in a concatenation of sea and sheepgrass,
and there is Frank with a yellowish suburb of Lima,
and Giant with an ever-changing —

And how, I cried as we hit the billowy-bouncing ice
of Pleasance 2 together like twins of Matti Haukamäki
on a good day, can a place be such places
altogether? amazed at the variousness of each all.

Ah ha, said the Pōhutukawa Tree, eternity requires
history and history that is
and history to come of each particular place
to be enough, and keep them in joy.

And so they were. And so it was.
Revolving 'midst the places that they loved
and will be home in.

We snowploughed to a kind of stop.
And now they revolved above us, now below,
and now we saw their hats, and now
their smiling faces, and now
some street of Melbourne, or some plain
of Kurdistan in all the beauty of being so loved.
Comparisons occur to me

because there are not words in men
plainly to show what has no words
made for it, for it is not,
yet it was.

Like neon butterflies, like seas made of cities,
like summer skies of forest robes,
like songs without words.

SONG 112 · *a little echo of dear Sam / leaving the twirling Lovers of Place / the
road to Pleasance 3 / what they saw upon the way / not stopping*

It becomes harder and harder of course,
as things less earthwise require the language
of loam and clay, but if I cannot go on,
I must go on, O Sam my friend.
Fail better: ha, it is such a good line,
though I have hopes of reaching my high end
in a blaze of ordinary invention.

Joy, bliss, happiness, how hard to describe,
against the knotted verve of darker energies.

Fuck a duck. Shit a brick.

The happy places faded on our sight
like dandelion clocks seen with amber glasses.

Twirling.
There is no movement more beautiful.

The dear Pōhutukawa Tree
poked me with his sledge-stick-twig
towards the pearl and diamond spiral
prinked with ruby flares along the way
to Pleasance 3, round, round, round, round,
and a little, past the third glass hillock, down.

Sweeeeesh! Sweeeeeeeeeeesh!

We had skied barely a minute or two,
which was, according to my soul's reckoning,
a thousand miles away from what I thought of
as being probably the correct answer, when —

Whaaaaaaa — ?

I made a serious effort at stopping,
for I had seen something approaching in the sky.
I would have said it was an angel, truly.
But the power of small metal edges
when travelling at the speed of light
is less than useful, and I skidded towards
the marmalade edge of the universe
in a heady spray of bergamotty ice-shavings.

SONG 113 · *the novice is rescued from falling / and wonders what day it is in Time / the flying Hakekeke described*

I was rescued by a bountiful branch
from the Pōhutukawa's selection,
which shot out several umber miles
and took me back within its golden-dusted,
scarlet-coronetted, barky arms.

Ta, I said.
No worries, said the tree.
We'll take that T-Symmetric trip, my friend,
when Sunday brings our Travels to their end,
the last few miles alone. Which made me cry,
but not from sadness. Sigh. Sigh. Sigh. Sigh. Sigh.
And would my sun and lakes and mountains look
a little grey, and tedious my book?

What day is it now?

There is no word for it.

Anyway, this angel-thing.
I am sure in my little lawn at Haast Beach
we would all think that it was one.
It was passing overhead with a small tattoo
and some genuine lambwhite. Flying,
it was of the posture of a jetpack man,
being upright but without a jetpack.
It appeared to tack and turn at will,
meaning by willing it, from the mind where else.

It was Hakekeke, from the Milk Powder Factory,
where we worked one summer in white flakes
and golden sunlight for bugger all really.
Where are you going? I cried.
To the Third Pleasance, where the Kind of Deed
are flying in great companies.

I asked the Tree, who was swinging his hips
in a kind of limbering up and down,
Are there no guides here, as there were below?
What need of guides, he replied leafily,
when the good way is already found?

SONG 114 · *a merry talk with Hakekeke / they follow her towards Pleasance 3 /*
the flying Kind of Deed in their squadrons draw near / oh what shall happen?

I can't wait I can't wait, said Hakekeke,
tipping sideways for mere dash,
and with a small whoosh
that made her white coat scudder,
and she like a flying sheep,
and just as lovely. Baa.

I shaded my eyes from the silver.
Tell me, I said to the hovering item,

141

do you know
what you did
in some mo
to be here?
Or can you see in the distance
the natural companions of your kind?

Yep. B-O-T-H.

Can you see them there flying. Just dots
in wee clusters like race-yawing yachts,
all toing and froing, all banking and bowing,
all oaring and soaring. Yup. Midge-thronging spots
that parted, convened, deployed and united,
like starlings at Otmoor, familiar-delighted,
and double in glee, at their glittering squall,
for flying with friends, and for flying at all.

Hakekeke zoomed about.
Come and see
at Pleasance 3!

As we sped over the saffron-scented snow,
hurling bow-waves of thick white crystal,
Hakekeke flew exultant upright above.
The soaring crowds grew nearer and nearer and nearer
and nearer, and the Tree gasped,
They come! They come! Get ready for
a Doppler Effect and an Inertial Frame Disintegration
nulli secundus, and a bloody great light!

SONG 115 · *a Physical consideration / a Linguistic consideration / a double-decker description of the Pass, and the glorious effect*

Two objects travelling at the speed of light
render the perception from the Inertial Frame
as 2 times c. This is ordinarily impossible.

What happened next was, to our limited conception here,
both inconceivable, and unfeasible.
And yet it happened, or how could I tell it you
and call it the Truth?

Our little glimmering band hastened breathlessly
down the ice; the nearing knots of Them
hummed, gargled, blared, then roared
towards us in a sky of sparkling kumqat zest.

Words are Truth for they are independent of us,
to be found apparently unused afresh by all
in dictionaries, thesauruses, lexicons and the like:
and they are Art for they are selected within us,
and moulded by our lives and souls, and chosen
in some mood, and for some purpose, known or hidden.

So here is the bloody test:
to tell you Truth and Art at once,
that you may know a Good Place
when you read one.

I plied my poles. The Tree centipeded his sledge.
Hakekeke willed her blissful speed.
Wham! We passed. Fuck me, excuse me,
They were singing. In fact, they had transformed
M, by now of course an impossible Mass, into Music.
It sounded a bit like an Manj-Tungu Goat-Calming Song.
And is the End of the Doppler Effect. It also glowed.
And our Inertial Frame fell to bloody bits, *splot,*
rendering E into Extasie, pregnant bankes,
violets, pillows, th'Atomies of which we grow,
sepulchrall statues and language understood;
and all became all minde by good love,
and were Unperplexed.
And the double of C became its square
in a bloody great light of Creation.

Thus: $\text{Extasie} = \text{Music} \times \text{Creation}^2$

The Kind of Deed wheeled about,
and accompanied us, with a lighter musical hiss,
over the glassy hillock to Pleasance 3.

I for one was buggered.
Even the dear Pōhutukawa Tree looked a little dangly.

Hakekeke flew into a cloud of friends
and passed across the lemon moon together.

We ploughed to a gentle stop.

I leaned against some proferred sugar branches.
We puffed and panted with sociable smiles.
Look! said the Tree.

Whilst the good folks whispered away by the moon
in a sky of billy-steam
and the spears of a million stars,
the corrugated-iron onion-domes of Pleasance 3
bobbed and undulated in their miles of brightness
like coloured lightbulbs crowded on a pleasant sea.
And from them some took off,
and amongst them some came in to land,
and somewheres they just softly tinkled.

And there are Ian and John! I cried,
glimpsing two soaring silhouettes
wafting in the auburn lights of evening,
who worked at the Kaikōura resurfacing!

Go up and speak to them, said the dear Pōhutukawa Tree.

And this, though it seem impossible,
is how I did just bloody that.

SONG 117 · *how the novice rose to Ian and John / and all their trialogue*

I hurried into the Beautiful City.
Its russet sponge streets. Its oak-bordered squares.
Its coppershine tenements.
Each with a hundred gold-lit windows.

And above, ah, where they flew,
its polychromatic chatoyance;
a vasty, leisured flibble of rainbows
borne from the bulbous domes of home.

As I bounced down Waitangi Street,
I felt the elastic extension of my stride,
both of the vertical and of the horizontal plane,
and soon I was looping along boing boing boing
in the arms of bearable prisms until
whoooo
        hooooo

I rose to the windows of gold,
I passed a raspberry dome,
and I flew
        ya-hoo!
my skis aflap,
to them.

Ahem.
How have I done this? I enquired,
aviating between the elbows of Ian and John.
You are still, they said with twinly unison,
not lost to the chance of a kindly deed.
Which was a kind of moral mechanics, I suppose,
and filled me, ah despitto Sam! with hope

and no little purpose.

With strained casualty I asked of them,
What had they done to be here?
And they replied, as we flit in a sequinned cloud,
that They had done a Kind Deed.
Which was not my news particularly,
And no matter which.

Together and swooping we landed in mother-of-pearl.
I knew that they knew that I would know as they knew
and know now, when I did thus.

SONG 118 · *the resting Tree / the novice looks back upon the Beautiful City /*
how beautiful it is / a thought or two / the Tree wakes / they ski down away

I bounced lessly and lessly back.
The Tree was resting in a halo of twinkles.
At each contented sigh of breath a sweet blizzard
of pollen, hushedly hay-gold, danced the Twist.

I had not the heart to wake him.

I crunched onto my arse for a break.
The glass slope was summer.
The Tree snorted softly.
My skis pointed at the cosmos.

I looked back drowsy at the Beautiful City.
In the reddled sky its citizens flew
in companies of joy, shaking hands in midair,
dancing of aerial hug and lips,
having thought of it, and done of it,
in their pointed lives.

Ah, how this would do, and be enough.

I determined to do good.
I knew I would know when I did if I could.

And how are the distractive matters of your busy lives?
For if our mechamisms do include
the lambent, airy cog of mansuetude,
what are we, to be merely bees about their hives?

Here, the Pōhutukawa Tree awoke and stretched,
with a homely creaking at his silvery joints.

A penny for your thoughts, he rumbled.
Shall we go on now, if you can imagine
anything better than this?

We chicky-chocked to our uprights.
And with a pole of stick and branch,
sped down about the civet-heliotroposity of ice and snow
towards the plug'ole, and the end.

SONG 119 · *what can be next? / they near the Slalom of the Brave / and enter its
course*

What is next and how can extasie be finer? I asked,
as we hurtled at an impossible music
towards the next rosy creation.

Like frozen lakes infused with Turkish thyme
and madder, the great-tongued landscape
juddered our skis as we swished and circled,
ever more tightly,
in our
spectacular
petallic
spiral.

Here comes a slalom that only the Brave
may perfectly pass, yelled the Tree with a wave

of his strengthiest boughs. I looked up ahead
through the curved, freshet world-wind, and Fuck me! I said,
for drawing at speedily near was a thicket
of whippy light-épées, whose serpentine snicket
looked bloody unlikely for anyone trav'lling
at our rocket-race, and whose intricate ravelling
resembled a bed of imagined-gold nails
in-woven (and out) with the icecreamy trails
of Those Who Were Brave and Permitted to Pass,
and Those Who Were Not And Fell Flat on Their Arse.

We whizzed at the first gold light-pole.

Red gate, blue gate, red gate, blue gate, said the Tree,
its foliage chattering in the whirlwind of our approach.
Remember the outside edge! Remember the pole-plant!
Beware the hairpin! Beware the flushes!

Too bloody late for all that cock.

Wham! I shouldered the first gate's first stick,
which was topped with a helpful little holograph
of a red ball, and sang *E Te Iwi E* in a lusty tenor.

Red   blue   red   blue
zip   zip

faster than you could say Waikikamukau

SONG 120 · *the Slalom song of the Pōhutukawa Tree / a sudden arrival / and a
fall / and a laugh*

I heard the Pōhutukawa Tree
twisting and turning
shouldering and barging behind me
with the noise of a tree slapping about
in a storm without so much
as a figure of speech.

I think he was singing too.

It was The Happy Wanderer
at twenty thousand r.p.m.

I was doing rather well,
considering the speed of light,
when I was overtaken by a youth on a snowboard.
Gidday, he said.

It was Kāmaka,
who had worked in the bakery at Rangiora,
with his unsurpassable Coffee Buns.
His racing posture was ophidian.
He pulled away in a split-second slither,
leaving only the liquid pour of his Ray-Bans,
and the scent of an improbable Merino
that had lived for some fair jacket.
Both momentary evanescences.

Distracted and unworthy,
I fell.

The Pōhutukawa Tree gnarled past me
singing Val-der-eee, Val-der-aaaa,
Val-der-eee, Val-der-a-hahahahaha!

And the Universe began to laugh.
Or was it me?
For it sounded small, like a human being.
Or an insect clinging to the silver chains that hung
down from the gorgeous cuckoo-clock
into eternity.

Her   her   her.

I picked myself up and completed the course.
My nether half subinfeudated from bendyrubberman
for the nonce.

Wibble whoosh wibble whoosh!

The youth Kāmaka the Brave
and the dear Pōhutukawa Tree
were sharing a pair of binoculars
bent upon some busy distance.
Bloody phew, I said, hams abloodytremble.

They turned to smile mewards,
in a slow spray of goldgleam and knightfizz.

Our dear friend here, said the tree,
winding a bough about brave Kāmaka's breast,
is bound to yon bright-bristling battle,
yon blow-braw bannerets –
here, youth blended its voice with the biomass,
and they sang together –
yon thunder-trumpeting,
yon air-bending drums,
and the passion-plumed pomp
of the persistent in Truth.

I thought I heard an allegorical neigh.
And perhaps through the diaphanous cream-ice
the jingle of curvettish snaffles
in a wind of wonder and faeryland.

Bloody stirring stuff.

And off, with a wave-scarf-scent of coffee buns,
rode Kāmaka, speeding to battle on his lime board.

What has he done to be here? I enquired.
Some majesty with kittens and mittens and snow,
said the Tree.

And we followed.
Would I see this great battle?
Fought by the already bold?

SONG 122 · *wheee! over the glassy mound to Pleasance 4 / they watch Kāmaka*
the Brave made a hero / and how he looked / and what it all may mean

Wheee! We propellered from the glassy mound.
It never as a pleasure palled.
But that is the matter of any kind of heaven.
We shot into the copper-lit gauze of highness.
Good things do not lack the glory of the Bad;
they are the best songs.

And scraped to a stop above a field
of a cloth of gold.

There he goes! rustled the tree.
And, indeed, youth shot into a drangly-thatched smithy,
like lime-lit lightning leaning lightly leftwards
wham!
where we heard a bing and a bong and a bang,
and saw a little spurticle of forge-fire,
and the dilly dump of a dung-drop,
and *wham-again!*
out he came,
in compleat gold harness, atop a prancing steed,
brandishing Elvirethilion at the golden sky,
and crying Truth! Truth! or was it Struth!

Upon his shield was the device of a Small Kitten,
couched versant in a mess of malachite mokimoki,
and upon his helm a small snow-making machine,

which blew its pale confetti-shiveriness
about his metal shoulders and the passing air.

And what does this mean? I asked the tree.
What knightly knowledge is here?

There is nothing like a symbol or two to make a man pause.

I know not, said the Pōhutukawa Tree.

And I could not be buggered to think of it myself.
In a good place the thinking is already done,
and enjoyment lies upon the look of things.

And, in the name of all that is good,
he looked like a bloody Hero.

SONG 123 · *the army of Courage and Truth described / and its Great Leader / and questions concerning Him answered*

A million mighty hoofbeats scrunched
the foil-flash of the cloth of gold,
in glittered panoply of proper pride.
And Youth galloped into their midst
with a sparkle of corslet and greaves.

It was an army all ahorse,
unbreakable in spirit and in flesh.
This is no sentimental stretch of human words:
they were unbreakable, and knew it,
flailing forth in blood and purpose
at the darkness in their van,
which I had seen before.

Great lines like ocean waves of gold,
champing mighty in their bridled prance,
the men and mounts, like souls and bodies bound,

clattered, caged their energy with winding noise,
and waited for the charge electric.

And at their head, stood in stirrups high,
the Tall Knight, clapp't in amber armour,
translucent to the starry sword-shine,
banners blowing from his basinet,
waved his crystal blade, whose light bored
the dark ahead with diamond drill-rays.

Surely, I said, more in awe than conversation,
that is some God, or an Angel at least.

Ho ho ho! cried the Tree. What need of Shades
invented out of fear? This is a man!
Forever-fearless, proud-of-purpose Man!

And he grew all orgulous-superb,
rattling from twiglets to twigs, to branches,
to boughs, to trunk and to crown,
spraying the gold-glinted cloud-rack with pollen
that spangled like starlight and moon-shake.

SONG 124 · *the symbols of the Tall Knight / their meaning / the novice asks to
go down amongst the army / they go down amongst the army / where they meet
Louey, Maui, Norma and Ollie*

For the Tall Knight carried a shield emblazoned
with two white stones in a fire in an oak on a calf
in a castle bedragonned with stars in a goblet;
and on his casque where all his banners blew,
a great ten-thousand-candle Lichtergestelle
turned its tinkling, clapping scenes of forest folk
amidst the hubbubbed army, lighting banks
of nodding sunflowers risen glorious from
the gardens on his spaulders on his shoulders.

I did not ask again about knightly knowledge,
for the meaning was clear and I do not need glasses.

Can we go down and be with them? I asked.
Soup-herb, said the tree, and we shot off.

Arriving, still ourselves, in a twinkling amongst
the pistoning pasterns and flummoxing fetlocks
of the horses of truth,
we herringboned about the golden field,
agawp at the splendour of brilliance near to burst,
and the clamour-crack, and the weapon-woof.

Surely there is some of the scrum of the
Brightwater Bigfoots that were! O Louey! O Maui!
O Norma! O Ollie! How did you get here, all armed,
from the playing fields of Centennial Park
and the year when we were all thirteen!

And they hefted their swords up and cheered
with a light in their mouths and tittup and piaff,
one hooker, one flanker, one lock and one prop:
All Hail! Wes thu hal! Clitter-clatter, clip-clop!

And I wept for my youth that had passed me
like truth on a snowboard:
the games and the after,
the bumps and the laughter,
all gone for a moment,
held here in Hope.

And out upon the bogged edges of the golden time
the enemy was ranged in ragged ranks of powder-blue,
all cloaked and hooded, blue of horse and helm,
and muttering with disappointment drear:

and all that I had seen –
battalions still-becalmed in blue cloakdrag,
squads of cleaved-plate breasts with blood-eyed hearts,
the helmless hordes of arrow-bonesplit heads,
mounted-mountain legions of flowed-over flesh agasp,
half-eaten cohorts of hog-toothed scabbage,
glass Immortals trembling with fear of death,
and the blind Myrmidons, hollow in armour of blue.

The Tall Knight raised Bright Biter.
The army of truth fell quiet.
A half-heard hoof-stamp.
The jingle of bridle and rein like a bell
far away and then gone.
One snort. One careful clatter.
One armour-joint.
And he spoke:

Folk without fear   in the world-fight
come at my calling   to courage and shatter
hold to your hearts   at the havoc of blood-fall
ride now ride   and reck not for ruin.

And lo! there was a gathering of muscle and thew,
and a facing of arms, and the reins loosed,
and the leaning forth, and the quake of the earth,
and the rending of gold underfoot,

and they were gone,
like a scurrying hedgehog

prickled with upraised blades.

Bloody Hell, I said.

I must remember to be brave
in truth in future.

SONG 126 · *they leave Pleasance 4 through a blizzard of golden seeds / the Song of the Seeds / the Song of the Seed Travellers*

We tittered back to the zoom-track,
and spiral-sped in the narrowing gyre
with melted light on my beanie,
in the company of some excited electrons.

Look! cried the Tree, Up ahead!

I looked up ahead.
A blizzard of golden seeds tinkled in our path,
like a gambolling game of golden cents.

We hurtled into their harvest,
and they sang, pittering about hoods and goggles,
in little, swirling, helium voices,
like the loosen'd ticks and tocks
of timeless clocks:

Touch us, touch us, Little John!

Which they kept repeating in various
perky, cutey and softyknob ways,
(Dutch uth dutch uth wittle Don /
Titch ooth titch ooth diddle Dom /
Tudge-iss tudge-iss liwwell Jin!)
which was not really a Song in my book.

And we sang back to the spattering,

darting gold-grain-sweetiepie-gnaticles
in our speedy merriness:

The orchard's green, the hops are high,
The shearers sing a lullaby,
The sun is up, the sky is blue,
And blossoms in the tawāpou!

And they crowded and parted,
zizzled and darted,
and cleped the way to Pleasance 5,

and I was glad to be alive!

SONG 127 · *they emerge at the glassy mound to Pleasance 5 / ooooop and thus remaining / the first view of the ships of the Menders of the Ways of Man*

Though of course to be dead
and here would be better
than a poke in the eye with a short stick.
Sharp stick.

We shot about a schuss-swerve
and saw before us a heliotropical tidal wave of ice,
which we were instantly upon
and as instantly off.

There was something unusual about our
parabola, our trajectory, our catenary:
my little knitted ski-jumper
whistled in its loomed and latticed rigging,
my corduroys snappled in a warmer wind,
and my great wood skis began to fluctuwag
in a gentle snoozy-snake, summer-seaswell
kind of way, while the dear Pōhutukawa Tree
sailed beside me upon the kindest, little-dipper air,
bestowing with its boughs its starry pollen

to the general day, downwards, where it floated,
droppingly, to the new geography of our perception.

The view of Pleasance 5 will be,
er, *aerial*, or *birds' eye*. See!
Down through the palmy, balmy mists,
The ships of the Philanthropists!

And sure enough, upon a lapis ocean drifted
barques, canoes, armadas, kayaks, galleys, lifted
lazy in the long Pacific, longships, bigrigs,
yawls and wherries, quinqueremes and luggers, bluebrigs,
jammers, clippers, packets, hoppers, please continue
according to your own acquaintance.

And far away,
but not too far,
the islands lay.

Mānawa.

SONG 128 · *the galleon of Poi and Queenie passes / an exchange of happiness*

We soared, oh how we soared.
The dear Tree taught me how to peer down
between the tips of my skis
so that I toppled neither left nor right
in my greedy joy of eye-feast.

At such breakneck velocity
I might have broken my neck
upon the air with such a twist.

Look! pointed the pointy Tree-branch.
Down there! A stately galleon
full of friends!

I saw upon the sea.
I saw the white ship-shape of foam.
I saw the wood-brown deck.
I saw the beetled bodies splaicing the bum-brace.
I saw the parallels to earth.
I saw the sails' broad bellies.
I saw the cannons' pates.
I saw the risen rigging.
I saw the mast-top pea.
I saw the golden gonfalons.
I saw the sunburned upturn faces two:
Poi and Queenie, I knew them,
who had been with me on the raft at Māpua,
so many summers sweet,
so many sweet ago.

And there, above the sun, we swapped
our happinesses, for they were the same.

SONG 129 · *Poi and Queenie sail away, singing of their early deaths / the novice sees a ship that nears an island / they go down*

And with a billow of gentle breezes,
their galleon tipped downwards at the blue,
where I saw its foam-fresh white oval
break upon the water, and heard their voices
singing in the heights:

they had fallen together off a mountain, which,
being of their deserved good place, peak-pointed
at the plughole we pursued even now,
meaning, thus, that as their crampons crackled
in uncertain footsure, they fell, in a puff
of dug-diamond crystal, upwards, tied together
and goggle-gape in liquid sunlight's gasp,
lifting limbs lightly, iceaxes flung in slowmo
at a cloud, and weightless packs spilling

torches, scroggin, carabinas, fleecehats,
dried apricots, jewel-hot water, arching arching
at the story
of their stones
and bones
and to their glory.

Let's go down, I cried at the twattering Tree.
For I had seen a ruddy randan butting at the beach
of some delicious isle.

Ah, adventure!

We leaned a little forward. Our bindings creaked.
We planed downwards.
An albatross slapped athwart us with a smile.
Things that I understood grew bigger.

SONG 130 · *they watch the crew of the good ship Reform disembark / the Tree*
explains what they will do / the visitors fly about for a general view

Crrrrrr-wisssssshhhh.

A beaky bow cleaved the yellow shore.
The quiet rowers raised the last-dip't oar.
They stepped across the shallows, passing, hand
To hand, their boxes, till they reached the land.

The ship creaked hushed upon the lapping tide.
The crew passed silent-smiled into the wide
And rustling greenness of the island wood.

The Tree swept like a star above them. Good,
he said, and nodded wisely. They will leave
themselves to make themselves a happy place,
and then sail on. Like Alexander did;
but without rapine and disdain.

And slipping slightly downwards still,
the sea a lapis glass for sharks and rays,
that lingered in their lying luxury,
we glided round the pattern of islands,
where folk lived well and ventured forth
both, like visions of themselves.

And scattered like opals on the sweetly burning sea
lay feluccas and galliots, spankers and tugboats,
gleaming punts and striped corsairs,
coming and going at once,
and multiplied with men.

In the act of wanting this, I believe I learned.

SONG 131 · *they land, exhausted, upon the ice and snow once more / a rest and a picnic / a talk and a snooze*

And doooooooon we came,
skiplane-skateroos,
into the tighter cone-centricity
of our accelerating tour,
landing like peas in a funnel,
crackitty-crakitty-crack, round and round,
but chatter-chatter-chatter to a halt.

Hurray. Pant gasp phew.

Time for a banana sandwich and a cup of tea,
said the dear Tree, humping off his little pack
and twiggling in its little depths.
He branched out a Minnie Mouse sandwich box
and a Gollum thermos.
Voir-lar, he said. I could not deny that I loved him.

We stood our skis in the snow under a lavender moon

and lay in the stripes of their lunar-scent shadows,
sucking our sandwiches
and sharing the slightly frightening thermos-top,
which stared at us from the brain-pool of its too-sweet tea.

Not far now, my friend,
Unto our timely end.
What will it be,
Pōhutukawa Tree?
Wait and see.

I lay back upon my oily parka
and waggled my ankles to prevent DVT.
The lavender light wandered in woggles
through my guide's leafage and branchage.

Sleeeeeeeep, he rustled.
We have all the … yaaaawn … time in the wor…

There are no dreams upon the nearness of perfection.
There is no other life when life is nuff.

SONG 132 · *they awake / and watch the arrival of Bush fed by the moon*

And we awoke refreshed.
Or extrafreshed. As we had not been tired.
Only a bit puffed.
Thus in goodness brightness builds itself
to some end.
Ah, what gusto, what great gusto!

The dear Tree finished his now-cold tea,
and smacked his leaves,
now greenside, now whiteside.
Righty-ho, he said, boughing himself vertical
in a staggering of multiple stilts.
To Rest Is Not To Conquer.

To which I acquiesce.
And rose from my arse and stretched
with crack-delicious, rack-auspicious, back-propitious
indiarubberinesses.

We stepped into our bindings.
Have a Mintie, said the Tree,
and we sucked sweet sweet whiteness
until, suddenly –

From out the ice in curling flosses,
Rose a floor of ferns and mosses,
Piupiu, Para, Whekī, Ponga,
Thicker, quicker, stronger, longer,
Next, twine-by them, shrubs and bushes,
Coiling up with little whooshes,
Followed by, but overtaking,
Stands of treelets, swooshing, shaking,
Stocks and boles and crowns appear,
Tōtara, Kahikatea,
Tawa, Rimu, Kauri, Rātā,
Mataī, Kāmahi, Taupata,
Rising in a symphony
Of lushy lumber, leaf and Tree,
And downy down the moonlight fed them,
Censed, conducted, spread and led them,
Bunched with birdies, tickled grubly,
Knobbly, bobbly, bubbly, stubbly,
Fruit and flower, bud and berry,
Tower and thicket, mighty-merry!

SONG 133 · *they superslalom through the bush / some moving moments
between Trees / the novice learns the difference between the sad simile and love*

Fuck me sideways, I said agrin.

Quietly, with a kind of rapt dignity,

distracted from me yet with love,
the dear Pōhutukawa Tree curled a branch
all candelabraed with crimson spicules
and speckled with silvery seed-salt,
about my duffelled bicep,
and set us gently off amongst his relatives.

We gained speed,
and yet his devoted abstraction remained,
turning to gaze at bush and bocage,
in awe too deep for show.

If this was not the best thing in the world
or out of it, then I am a monkey's uncle.
And yet something still to go.

You know how skaters skate in double bliss,
With crosséd arms and sympathetic hiss,
Their rhythmic lefts and rights the swaying song
Of sweet propulsion, loving, hushed and strong?
Well, so we did. And through the flickered trees,
All-ushered by a Golden Syrup breeze,
We took our way; and as we passed the leaves
Of friendly flora high-fived at my sleeves
And blushcheeks, and my guide slapped softly back,
And wept to be so joy-jacked.
                                    And my pack
glowed like the moon and the sun were in it,
and the canvas weft translucented, and the buckles
gleamed like the bones of hope burned in a furnace.

And the bush was not sucked to me selfishly,
in the cosmic similes of small-man-comfort,
but I, *er*, gave myself, in, *ahem* …

universal love.

I blush at such words,
with reddened joy.

From between a stately passing grove of Porokaiwhiri
appeared a pair of equally accomplished superslalomites,
travelling also at the speed of light,
with stars on springs on headbands on their heads.

Giddaaaaaaaaaaaaaaaaaaaaaaaaay, they called,
swerving into our green direction,
and paralleling every skate with ours.

Surely you are Ricky,
Surely you are Solomon,
Who came with me from Babylon to Tyre,
and shared our bloody chickpeas and t-shirts,
and parted in the fireworks, beer and chicken
by the ink-bright sea?

Yeah right, they said together,
a little sly acceleration winking at their words,
which distracted the Tree for a splittest second,
for which he was slapped in the seed-pod
by a chuckle-Hīnau, and turned determined.

We leaned a little forth, and pushed at our edges,
and drew alongside, ferns flapping at our socks.
Our speeds increased so that our masses reversed
into tending lightness. Faster, faster, faster,
our octo-plank-sleigh whizzed in the woodgreen.
They giggled. We giggled. For the tree, a kind of bark.
Lighter, lighter, we thrust through the bushline
and whoooooa! flew from the grass-glassy mound
into an aerial circus, our quadrotor-heavenlycopter.

We cleared a chalcedony river,
and a porphyry plain.

That's us, said Solomon.
There, said Ricky.

It was only a garden.
But, oh, what a one.

SONG 135 · *they land all together in the Garden of the Kind / Ricky and Solomon go to their perfect work / the novice wanders, skiless, in the wonder / he considers the sympathy of Nature and Man*

We landed in it, thump, bump, clump, dump,
I in a thicklet of purepink kākābeak,
which took me like a mattress,
threw me back up a little, caught me,
laid me down, and arranged itself around my warmwear
with a small aaark and a waft of honey-on-toast.
The dear Tree, still in ecstasy,
was slapped softly about with a spray of harakeke,
and a tui throat-bobbing bewilderments from its apparent ears.
Burbleburble kweek kweek.
Here, said my friends, unclipping their skis
and standing them in a wigwam among mountain daisies,
we shall tend to our garden.
And as you tended to Man, boomed the Tree
from his heaven of touch-tickle flax-sparkle,
so shall he blossom and sprout, blossom and sprout.

I waved them goodbye.
The Tree snoozed in his relatives.
So I wandered away, wondering wherever I went.
My skis stood at the skyline like a chalet door
without a chalet. I have always thought
that Nature was no part of man,
unless by our invented need to have it part of us.
I have always thought
that in its blind, mechanic round,
nobility and beauty, intricate and grand,

it had nothing for its other selves, but only us,
and only that because these words were ours.
But here ... Ah, but here, the needed dream
that we are one was all before my eyes.

The blest passed, in infinite landscape
peopled with plants and birds, from hill to valley,
saddle and ridge to river-flat and scree,
beach to mountainside, field to bush,
in shining sympathy with all that lived.

Could I believe, now,
that we were made for each other,
not by a master's hand, but out of ourselves?

SONG 136 · *the novice encounters a vegetable sheep / and a wandering Charitable Comforter / they look out from a mountain ridge into all of Pleasance 6*

It looked a little like home.

I stomped up a windy ridge.
A whistling pipe in a cairn of stones whistled the way.
I came upon a vegetable sheep,
decorated with a kea.

Quwaaaark, said the kea.
And the vegetable sheep suggested
the comforts of beauty.
What I suggested to it, who on earth could know.
What reward was this!
The kea appeared interested in my bootlaces.
I entertained him for a while with thoughts
of the consolations of muscosity.
He nibbled and bobbed with a beady eye.

Up upon the slightly snowy saddle stood a figure
clapped in armour, surveying the garden-globe.

I watched him, unmoving as he was, for a while.
Then I scrabbled to my feet and puffed to his place,
and stood at his side near the top of this world.

And on the slopes and lower land
Grew plants and flowers that understand,
Tended by the quiet-kind,
As balsams for the human mind,
Whose vastness and variety
Lay still in every bush and tree.

The cloak of my companion flapped.
The kea waited on the Haastia cushion.
I knew this was another world.
Sam would have died at its fiction.

SONG 137 · *the novice returns to the tree through an apple orchard / the Tree*
chooses to stay / the novice leaves for Pleasance 7 upon his directions

I returned though an orchard of Southern Snap.
Each little red-green world turned
with a shiny reflection of those who had passed.
I walked amongst kindness in wimples and wellingtons,
codpieces, coat-tails, jackets and pixieboots,
tabards, chemises, bloomers and zoot-suits,
sliding about and about the apple-skin,
round and round like the earth
made of flesh and juice
and the seed in Castle Core.

The dear Pōhutukawa Tree had risen from his flax,
and was holding our skis in his twiglets.
Guess what I saw! I cried.
A kiwi kooking kabbage in the kitchen, said the Tree.
And all about, toetoes frothed and rattled.

So to the long last place,

whose eternal hope I hoped for.

That's it for me, said my Tree.
Here, where we have conveniently joined
in some soft purple fantastical philosophy,
we shall part. This is my place.

Which was as obvious as obvious can be.
He handed me my skis. I snapped them to.
I took my poles and slapped about a bit,
wondering what embrace or kiss or words
might
be right.

Follow the buttercups, said the Pōhutukawa tree.
They will take you to the field of wheat.
And on its other side the highest good
dances in its human multitude.

A wave turned out to be best.
I saw myself in a bunch of grapes,
manyness and alone.

SONG 138 · *he proceeds alone to the faded wheatfield at the edge of Pleasance 7 /*
and starts through it / wheat

Buttercup, buttercup,
Do you like butter,
Giddyup, giddyup,
Jump in the gutter.

I skipped along on my skis,
amidst the brilliant-yellow hula-hoops
of reeling petal-packs.

I was not exactly afraid.
To draw near the highest happiness

can only make one wish to stay,
and when one cannot, as I could not,
determined to win it for later.

A little unworthy nervousness,
both of the present and of the efforts to come
in the years that were left to me,
was all that leaked about my heart.
I saw the wheatfield ahead.

I poled along in cross-country style,
and entered the harvest field with a swish
like a swimmer breasting the salt and the waves
of an old-gold sea: for the wheat was faded,
and a cardboardy colour, drooping its ears
like too-loaded purses, weary and ripe.

Flour flew into the sky,
and I sped in a curious charity:
for what was wheat but a plant
that had found its salvation
by finding that man had its use,
and making itself to that end.

Which cheered me up,
for ripeness is all,
though it look past its best.

SONG 139 · *the novice reaches the end of wheat / the view / he leaves his skis and begins to walk on / he hears music / and meets the Pilgrims of the Pleasance*

One stalk, crippled and sulphur-shone,
loaded like a broken wand, was the last.
It dangle-dusted downward,
looking for something in the earth of ice.

I had finished the field.

Before me stretched a pleasing prospect
of low green hills, curling mathematically
into a tightness, like a painted landscape
whose conoided canvas is a trumpet.

These, the slower mounds of entry to the last Pleasance,
looked like nothing for my skis, and so I left them,
as near the woody world where they belonged as I could do.

I marched into the ferny pastures.
A little trod-track showed the way.
A titter of sheep-hoofs pressed it into brownness.
Droppings shone like olives.

Stopping to consider a particularly fragrant taramea,
I caught the tiny howl of a coven of cats.
I cupped my large ears in their direction.
They were suspiciously rhythmic.
Was this where I was bound?
To fill the sounding bits of this far melody?
I flapped forth, seeming, just a little,
to stay in the air with tiny ecstasy at each bound.

Suddenly, round the corner, which was not a corner,
but the nondegenerative coordinate of a conical section,
appeared a little line of dancing loons,
dressed in motley. They were,
by another little brown elliptical axis,
predestinated to cross my path, and join me,
in a mere moment.

Which they did,
cavorting carolly.

We stopped and stared at each other for a bit.

Surely, said one of them,
nodding his painted papier-mache horsehead,
that is John! Who …
Surely, said another, a cardboarded cockerel,
and a little nearer now,
we used to …
Surely, said a third, with a pigsnout
hammered of a beantin, elastically fitted,
it was at …
Surely, said the last, sporting a wekahead
made out of raffia and plastic rulers,
you are …

Oh, Just Visiting, I said, looking rather normal
in this company. Not dead yet.

They thought this indescribably funny,
and laughed like horns.

I'm Tommy, said the horse, winding his hands
in a fair imitation of rearing.
And this is Una (who was the rooster),
And this is Vic (who was the pig),
And this is Witi (who was the weka).

Do I know you? I asked.

Ah, said the pig, we shall all be welcome
at the Fair.

Which seemed to me to mean more than it did.

With a chook and a nag to my left,
and a weka and a porker to my right,
we set off, wideways, holding hands,
hornpiping halong the haway,

up and down the lovely hills,
they kindly giving me the track to dance down.

The airy music began to fill in its own spaces,
and began to be bagpipes, bellow-bright asquawk.

SONG 141 · *they reach Pleasance 7 / the Festival-Fair of Good Faith / things fall away*

Tralala, down we doowopped, jigwise and jollily.

Something flew off me wheee!

Bounce-bounce down the brackenway.

Something else flew off me whooahohoho!

The bagpipes blew brawly over the banks.

Hoofed, trottered and wing-winged, I came to the Fair.

Something moved more-away: flying like necklaces lifted.

And golden sunset's Schubert glow.

We stopped upon a windmill hill.

My animals of paste and paper cried Hello!

And can you guess what lay before us in the setting light?

The honking merriment of Man.

Whose something something something work was done.

And was it for today, or some fled season?

And now to be together something was his something bliss.

Ah, I have it!

Something flew from me now, like a gilt-baroque scab.

And I saw with the freshness of blood!

Come on! I cried. For Sam and for Joy! For the dear Treeeeee!

And we charged into happiness, bagpipes and potage.

Whoop-bloody-eeeeeeeeeeeeeeee!

SONG 142 · *the Festival and Fair of Good Faith described / and joined in*

Ah, it all became clear.
In the manner of getting new glasses.
Or a blood transfusion.

The hónkíng mérrímént of mán,
Whóse bríght, résígned, méchánick wórk
Fór óne móre dáy wás done –
Hay!

(Now you may stamp on at your dance
to what beat you imagine or please.)

And now to be together only,
Now to be together only,
Was his very bliss –
Hay!

(The horse galloped amidst the sweaty swell,
and bore two clodhoppers to their ale.)

The Fairly happy undeceived,
the fairly happy undeceived,
Roaring 'bout their pleasure –

Hay!

(And the pig wobbled forth at the mess,
and toppled the tapsters and potboys haha.)

The ruminant autumnal-merry
Roominant ortumnill-merrie
Golden wayzgoose-time –
Hay!

(And the weka charged through the danced mud
and bit all the bootstrings unknotted hoho.)

Where folks in smocks and beanies bouncing,
Bouncing brave on common benches,
Stuffed their faces full –
Hay!

(And the rooster clattered onto a vasty trestle
and cock-a-doodle-dooed on the bagpipe-twiddle.)

SONG 143 · *more of the same*

Pancakes, popcorn, peasey-pudding,
Parsnips, pizzas, port and pop,
O Stuffed their faces full –
Yay!

(And I ran to the mishmash with a mouth full of music,
and limbs lithe-loose with delight of the dance!)

And Little Titch and Sweet Maid Nut,
Asinging-dancing hiphophip,
And five of us among –
Yay!

(And there are Xavier and Yolande frolicking here!

To be seven. To be seven and all.)

And fat in codpiece-placket near,
In cock and cunt vicinity,
All to the bagpipe band –
Yay!

(And I wish there were Sam, a little apart, oh, but here too,
upon a dunghill smiling at fatuity.)

And some in windows, red and chortled,
Entered from behind at windows,
By some half-lit bumpkin –
Yay!

(And the man dressed in cats, and the Contralto Piharau,
and the glow-worms, and L the unhappiest tree.)

The village trees wave gilded branches,
Gilded branches at their junket,
And far away the hills –
Yay!

(I wish they could all be here. I wish that I will be.
But that is another matter, and unsettled yet.)

The purple hills of heather glow
With all that we could well expect
from this brief simple life –
Yay!

SONG 144 · *the novice and his friends enjoy themselves / the groot bleck blint
goes up behind / the full circle done with a vision of the damned*

I watched them my friends
grow tired with laughter and ebullition.
And they fell in drunken sleeps

decorated with ribbons and whirligigs.

And I danced till the sun went away
and the moon rose and the night-horn blew
with a sad-sweet note like two harmonick cows.

And at that moment the painted sky,
its lowering cloudrack and last-scarlet skin,
its silhouette-treearms, and light-learning stars,
began to draw up from the ground like…

a great black blind – ah! a grite block blend! –

this was no simile, my dear friends.

And slowly, from their socks and upwards,
came the damned:
                    who watched the world
that they had lost for their deluded braver sky
that never was, and in the slothful death of their courage
to bear the life that cannot be borne, that is all ours!

And still it wound slowly upwards,
the whole world's safety curtain, black and blind.

The whole front faces of the godmeant damned,
like tourists at a Tioman sunset,
burning burning more more higher higher
gilded angel-bright and horrorstruck,
and dark and cold behind.

And ripped their bloody hearts with rue.

I had made a circle full.

And they stared, and I stared,
and I danced into sleep,
and they stared at me dancing into sleep,
and my eyelids came down as the grit bluck blond came down,
and we fell to our lives,
I through the rose's white centre,
they to their awful attention.

Did I really truly honestly fall through a pea in a cone,
and pass through a blue-gridded map of always,
without Tree, without Joy, without Sam,
and land on the mountain once again,
above the glittered lake?

What a stupid bloody question!

My iPad said it was Sunday.
Somewhere there might have been
a kind of fat, imagined peace.
But here the little launches flickered in the water.
The keas scrabbled on the corrugated-iron roof
of the hut. Tiny insects shuttled about in the tussock.
Little scree-scraps tumbled clicketty-click
over the side of the ridge. Wind blew in the mānuka.
Water drip drip dripped into the plastic barrel.

And, suddenly, I knew I needed people.

I clapped on my headphones
and started down the track.

So where was Zippy? The last, lovely friend?
Had he not died yet? Had he chances still
to be good? Would his every atom of time

be given to its eternal place? Would I see him again?
Was I really nearly home? Would there be people there still?
Or were they all gone to their longer lives?

The answer was probably: all.

SONG 146 · *the novice descends the mountain*

I tramped on the skull of the earth.
Fried eggs for tea.
The track was narrow and worn deep
into the grey erosion of the mountainside.
It wound down in zigzags,
and flowed out around a promontory,
and back towards Cup Creek.

Where I took the cup from the nail in the tree
and bent to the little, steep creek that tumbled
down from the top of the mountain
through its bare and dusty channel,
and took up one white enamel cupful
of water. Here my father had drunk.
My mother. My brother. My friends and relations.
Acquaintances. Strangers. Dead men and deader.
The going, the going and the gone.

And I drank, and put the cup back on its nail.
And here they would drink who came next,
and next after that, and those so far after
they could not be imagined, if the mountain
had not fallen by now, rattling eroded into the lake,
and pushing bright, clear water gently
up the trunks of trees to their crowns,
which would wave and drown to nothing,
with Man long gone.

And the wheat that loved Him would wave,

and only the lives in the places I saw
would be left. For we are seas,
and for our own salt die.

Fried eggs from the pan.
Tea from the billycan.
Icecream and jelly.
Some crap on the telly.

SONG 147 · *song 147*

Little book, farewell.
Be it Heaven or Hell.

Come my dear friends all.
And take your curtain-call:

A, B, C, D, E, F, G, H, I, J, K, L, M, N, O, P, Q, R, S, T, U, V, W, X, Y, Z;
bow
Ay, Bee, Cee, Dee, Eee, Eff, Gee, Aitch, Eye, Jay, Kay, Elle, Em, Enn,
Oh, Pee, Queue, Are, Ess, Tee, You, Vee, Dubblew, Exe, Why, Zed;
bow-wow
Adam, Beatrice, Charlie, Dawn, Etera, Frank, Giant, Hakekeke, Ian,
John, Kamaka, Louey, Maui, Norma, Ollie, Poi, Queenie, Ricky,
Solomon, Tommy, Una, Vic, Witi, Xavier, Yolande, Zippy;
bow-wow-wow
the deer, the rabbits, the peacocks, koromikos, mozzies, tuataras,
    titiwais, wētās,
horse-stingers, karakas, giraffe weevils, butterflies, camels, beetles,
    whakahās,
matuku-moanas, tuis, albatrosses, dolphins, sharks, cats, kākās,
    kehas, piharau,
kāruhiruhi, katipōs, kōkakos, whai repos, kōtares, kingfishers,
    pāpahus, lambs, merinos, pūtangitangis;
clap clap clap
The Vegetable Ewe, The Pūkeko in a Fez, the Pūriri Moth,
The Winsome Weka, The Golden Kiwi, The Snapping Shrimp,
    Lineout;

encore encore
The Bloody Great Liar, The Becapped Woman, The Nudist,
The Quite Good Man, The Tall Knight;
applawse applawse
Sam, Joy, the dear Pōhutukawa Tree,
and me;
to the rafters.

Now put all things away.
The sun shines bright on Golden Bay.

THE END